OTHER COMMUNIONS OF JESUS

-Eating and Drinking the Good News Way!

JOHN HENSON

O Books is an imprint of John Hunt Publishing Ltd., The Bothy, Deershot Lodge, Park Lane, Ropley, Hants, SO24 0BE, UK
office@johnhunt-publishing.com
www.O-books.net

Distribution in:

UK
Orca Book Services
orders@orcabookservices.co.uk
Tel: 01202 665432 Fax: 01202 666219 Int. code (44)

USA and Canada
NBN
custserv@nbnbooks.com
Tel: 1 800 462 6420 Fax: 1 800 338 4550

Australia
Brumby Books
sales@brumbybooks.com
Tel: 61 3 9761 5535 Fax: 61 3 9761 7095

New Zealand
Peaceful Living
books@peaceful-living.co.nz
Tel: 64 7 57 18105 Fax: 64 7 57 18513

Singapore
STP
davidbuckland@tlp.com.sg
Tel: 65 6276 Fax: 65 6276 7119

South Africa
Alternative Books
altbook@global.co.za
Tel: 27 011 792 7730 Fax: 27 011 972 7787

Design of text and cover: BookDesign™, London

ISBN 1 905047 49 5

A CIP catalogue record for this book is available from the British Library.

Printed in the USA by Maple-Vail Manufacturing Group

OTHER COMMUNIONS OF JESUS

-Eating and Drinking the Good News Way!

John Henson

BOOKS

WINCHESTER UK
NEW YORK USA

CONTENTS

Preface

THIS volume represents one of a trilogy, the first to be published (1994). 'Other Temptations of Jesus', though conceived first, was published in 2004 as the Archbishop of Canterbury's Recommended Lent Book. The third, in preparation, will be 'Other Prayers of Jesus'.

'Other Communions' has influenced the thinking of a substantial number of progressive Christians since its first publication, including students at theological colleges. It is time to make this study available again so that those who have not previously been aware of its existence may have the opportunity to be informed and challenged by it. The material is at one and the same time scholarly, devotional and practical. Some of John Henson's 'Buttons Polished' (i.e. updated hymns) are introduced in the sections. In the appendices are patterns for experimental liturgies.

John Henson is now best known for his work on the 'Good As New' version of the Christian Scriptures, which he accomplished in community with the radical network 'ONE for Christian Exploration.' His other works include 'The Bad Acts of the Apostles' (1995) and 'Gems Reset and Buttons Polished' (1999)

This edition of 'Other Communions', John wishes to dedicate to his family, now seventeen strong, who all live nearby, and who give him a lot of love and support, namely Valerie his wife, their children and partners – Gareth, Sarah, Iestyn, Liz, Rhoda, Gary; and grandchildren- Aidan, Bleddyn, Carys, Gwenllian, Dyfrig, Iona, Isobel, Tomos and Ffion-Medi.

INTRODUCTION

THE idea suggested by the title of these studies, that Jesus on more occasions than just one celebrated Holy Communion (Eucharist, Mass, Christ's Supper, Breaking of Bread etc) during his earthly ministry may come as a surprise to some, cause anger to others and annoyance in yet others. Some may be annoyed by yet another attempt to comb the scriptures in pursuit of scant evidence for a dotty thesis. Those angry will be so probably because the forms of theology of Holy Communion that they have received through their particular tradition they regard as authoritative and final except perhaps in minor detail, and the possibility of a major shift in emphasis with scriptural backing will pose a threat.

Our practice, if not our theology of holy communion is derived almost exclusively from the Institution of Christ's Supper, which took place on the night of the betrayal of Jesus, in the Upper Room, as recorded by Paul in his first letter to the Christians of Corinth (11: 23-26). This account has special authority in that it is the earliest account of the eucharistic meal in the Christian scriptures- earlier than the accounts recorded in the gospels Mark, Matthew and Luke. The claim of Paul to have received the tradition from the Leader himself (whatever that may mean) has also to be taken seriously. But Paul, as always, was addressing a particular situation in a particular Christian community. Much of Paul's teaching intended for the particular has been applied to the general with less than happy results. The celebration of Christ's Supper or the Agape (= 'love-feast'; probably there was no clear distinction between the two at the time) was, at Corinth, chaotic, blasphemous and quite un-Christian. There was over indulgence by some, and the food communally provided to ensure that the poorer Christians received a square meal, was unfairly shared. Paul's answer was to sound the solemn note by informing the Corinthian Christians of the words of Jesus spoken on his betrayal night, which indicated that the sharing of the elements was to be in remembrance of his death and therefore not an occasion for riotous behaviour. This he coupled with warnings against eating and drinking unworthily. (Judas is not mentioned, but his shade is invoked.) Paul's advice in this particular situation where things had got out of hand was that normal eating and drinking should be done at home and that the remembrance of Christ's death in the ritual of bread and cup be a solemn and formal occasion within the worship of the Church.

If the Corinthians were immediately obedient to Paul's instructions, we can imagine agape features being stripped away from Christ's Supper and something like our ordered celebrations emerging, especially since they now had a liturgy to hand contained in Paul's account of the institution. Where this left the poor one can only speculate, but it is difficult to imagine they were better off as a result of Paul's advice, eating and drinking in their own homes instead of having the sporting chance of picking up a good meal in the fellowship of the church. The pattern laid down for Corinth was probably gradually adopted by other churches, especially as copies of Paul's letters came to be passed around. Thus a solemnifying of the feast came about in communities where perhaps Paul's strict line was less needed than in Corinth. Even in his letter, Paul shows he is aware that Christ's Supper does not exclusively celebrate the death of Jesus. The words 'until he comes' point to that aspect which is an anticipatory celebration of final victory and the banquet of God's New World (The Kingdom). However it looks as if Paul may have been responsible, probably unintentionally, for the strong emphasis placed on the death of Jesus in our celebrations of Christ's Supper, especially in western Christendom, almost, but not quite, to the exclusion of other aspects. Our own narrow literalism and our emotional need to have things neat and tidy has led us all to fasten on to Paul's order – to go with him to the Upper Room and to stay there behind locked doors. Mark, Luke and Matthew follow suit. By the time they came to be written there would have been time for the Pauline pattern to become widely established and thus, even if the gospel writers draw on separate remembrances of what took place on that fatal night, they would also by then have in mind the liturgical need of the Church for an ordered pattern of eucharist on the lines that Paul intended. This concern is especially the case in Matthew.

But was Paul's account of what happened in the Upper Room the sole origin of Christ's Supper? Was Paul's line so direct and hot to Jesus that no other lines can be imagined to exist? Paul does not actually say, 'I am now giving you the institution of Christ's Supper'. That is what we have said he is doing – it is a fair interpretation in the context. But an equally fair interpretation would be that Paul is simply saying, 'This is what I know for a fact to have happened on the night Jesus was betrayed'. 'In particular, on that night, one of the disciples partook unworthily and made a mockery of the communion. Make sure you don't do the same!'

The Corinthian Christians were already celebrating Christ's Supper, albeit unworthily, before Paul sent his letter. Where did they get their customs and practices from? From Paul's missionary foundation of the church? If so, why were they not doing things properly? Had they lapsed? Or had Paul not given them the teaching he now gives them? He seems, against the background of what is their present practice, to be advocating a quite radical reform, for which, nevertheless, he claims the authority of Jesus himself. Had he only just had revealed to him in some kind of vision of Christ the significance of the Upper Room communion, whose details he would have probably had from one of the friends of Jesus who had been present?

The communal meal was an important feature of the life of the first Christians. They had 'all things in common' (Acts 3:43ff) and to break bread together from house to house must have been the central act of their unity, as fundamental as it was common. It is pointless to ask whether this 'breaking of bread' was agape or Christ's Supper. Jesus must have been remembered at every meal – indeed, in this charismatic (excitingly spiritual) and eschatological (looking to the end of time) community, he was never forgotten. The circumstances of his death were very close in terms of time and the sense of his risen presence was not a pious hope but a reality, since within the community were many witnesses of his resurrection who would have been thrilled, but not surprised, had he walked through the door as he had dome only quite recently. However hard we try we cannot capture that immediate sense of Christ's presence that was uniquely theirs. The idea of Paul receiving guidance from a direct face to face interview with Jesus is difficult for us, but not for the first Christians. Rocky (Peter) and others had had similar interviews a short time previously.

For the origin of the sacred meal as the centre-piece of Christian life and worship it is best to begin with an appreciation of the importance of shared food in eastern culture. In the east, to share food with another, be it only humble salt, produces a bond of friendship that is sacred. In the west, despite the fact that eating and drinking plays its part in socializing, it is difficult to capture the strength of this feeling. The nearest equivalent in terms of bonding would be our society's traditional feelings about shared sex as an event that sacramentally joins two people together in an extreme and unbreakable way. Since such sentiments are now cherished with decreasing tenacity only by an unfashionable minority in our society, we cannot even cite sex as a telling comparison.

One of the best examples of the significance of the common meal as a bond is the story of the Gibeonites in Joshua 9. In order to escape the Israelite 'ban', which entailed the extermination of conquered peoples, the Gibeonites disguised themselves as wandering beggars. In accordance with the customs of hospitality to strangers they were received and food was accepted from their hands. As a result of this food-sharing, which embodied a treaty of friendship, they could not be exterminated when the truth was revealed. Though by trickery, they were now kith and kin to the Israelites. Joshua avenged the trick by giving them the status of 'hewers of wood and drawers of water'.

Only against this kind of feeling can the indignation of the first Christians against the action of Judas be understood. They were put in mind of Psalm 41:9 'Someone shared my food, then kicked me.' (John 13:18 Good-as-New)

Jesus and his disciples followed the practice of other groups of pious Israelites bound together by some shared interpretation of the Law or hope for the future, in eating and drinking together in this understood and accepted bond-cementing way. The description of God's New World as a feast and the open invitation to others to join in, is an important theme in the teachings of Jesus. Frequently it is linked with a picture of himself as the Bridegroom, and those responding to this appeal are the guests of the Bridegroom. The feast is a wedding banquet and thus definitely not a time for mourning. A wedding is a time of rejoicing and also a time of hope. The friends of Jesus cannot, like the Strict Set (Pharisees), indulge in fasting, for the Bridegroom is with them and the guests at a wedding do not go without food. (Mark 2: 18 & 19). The picture of Jesus as the Bridegroom, and the Messianic age as a banquet, is one which persisted in the communities of the first Christians (Revelation 21:9 & 19:9) Jesus's acceptance of invitations to dine with the most dubious of characters and the consequent disgust of the Strict Set must also be understood against this background. Nowhere does Jesus so justly earn the title 'Friend of Sinners' than in his willingness to sit at the same table with them. (Mark 2:15 & 16; also Matthew 11:19; Luke 19: 7. Stories about feasting: Matthew 22: 1-10; Luke 14: 15-21; Luke 15: 22ff; Matthew 25: 1-12; Matthew 8:11)

The sacred meal formed an important part of the Jewish sacrificial system. The primitive idea behind such meals was that both God and worshipper shared the same food and so were bound in a relationship of friendship or covenant with one another. The Passover meal was one such occasion. The Passover lamb, sacrificed to God in the Temple, was later shared by the Jewish family in a feast of remembrance. Thus table and altar are linked, and each pious family group with father at its head was a microcosmos of the holy people of Israel whose leader and parent was God. The covenant relationship is thus re-enacted and reaffirmed in every loyal home.

Jesus and his disciples, like similar groups of disciples, acted as a family, and as a family celebrated the Passover Meal. Even without the special words of Jesus in the Upstairs Room proclaiming the New Covenant, for the Christian with hindsight the picture of Jesus eating with his friends must in itself produce its own train of thought. The God thought of as present with his people through sacrifice and sacred meal is now present **in the flesh** and presides at the meal in person. From God's own hands and not from the hands of any priest or officiant, the friends received the food and drink. In reality and not just symbolically, the life of God and the life of God's friends entwine and transfuse each other.

Thoughts such as these have inspired these studies whose prime purpose is devotional. The scholarship is not watertight. I hold the view that we have insufficient evidence either in terms of documents or knowledge of first century culture to do any more than guess at the practices of the first Christians. It is unlikely that there was anything approaching complete uniformity. I hope there may be spiritual insights in these studies that will add to our appreciation of Christ's Supper. It is not my object to cancel out other insights but rather to add to them. To stress the aspects of life and Resurrection in Holy Communion is not to deny the eternal remembrance of and gratitude for Christ's sufferings and death. Nor to stress the aspects of Jesus's daring and shocking communion with sinners while yet in their sinful state (which the Church still finds it as difficult as did the Pharisees to swallow) is it to deny those aspects of consecration and commitment that are also present.

If, as a result of these studies, Christ's Supper for someone contains more joy and more of the sense of release from the oppression of guilt; if above all there is a greater sense of the reality of the presence of the risen and all-loving Christ, I am content.

THE CRITERIA

How many communion services are to be found in the gospels? The answer will depend on what your view of a communion is. But should not our thinking be the other way round? Should not our view of the communion service depend rather on those recorded incidents in the life of Jesus that appear to foreshadow it? – those occasions when Jesus sat at table, or sometimes without a table, and ate and drank in fellowship (communion) with other people. Shall we say that some such occasions cannot relate to the practice of Christ's Supper because our ecclesiastical rules do not appear to apply? Eating and drinking that do not take place within hallowed walls, in which there is carelessness with regard to the credentials of servers and recipients, to say nothing of table manners – how can anyone suggest that they constitute an observance of Holy Communion? Ought we not rather to ask, how can our observances of The Jesus

Meal be truly such if they ignore the principles and practices, indeed the spirit of those occasions when Jesus ate and drank with people in his day? Do we stick fast to Paul's account of the words and institution of Christ's Supper and shut out every other breaking of bread by Jesus to which the gospel writers bear witness because Paul's account resembles most closely communion as we understand it and wish to confine it? Or dare we allow the light from Jesus himself to illuminate and enrich the important witness of Paul?

In identifying the communion services of Jesus I have adopted three basic criteria. They are criteria all would regard as essential for a celebration of Holy Communion. They may be regarded as arbitrary only in the sense that they may be considered by some to be insufficient. This must be a matter of opinion. I hope to convince. The criteria I have adopted are these:-

1. THE PRESENCE OF JESUS

This is the central reality of Christ's Supper. Not remembrance, not sacrifice or thanksgiving, nor commitment nor unity – all of which are relevant and play their part.

Thy presence makes the feast;
Now let our spirits feel
The glory not to be expressed,
The joy unspeakable.

(Charles Wesley)

The doctrine of the 'Real Presence' – how it is defined, in what sense is Jesus present in Holy Communion, has been the source of the greatest division within the Church. When Jesus walked in Galilee his friends were spared this debate. He was present, could be seen, heard and touched. To be with Jesus, to eat and drink, and to do everything else with him that comes within the bounds of common human experience – this was the unique privilege of the first century inhabitants of The Middle East. Only in the Resurrection communions do doubts begin to arise and we see already beginning to germinate the seeds of the difficulty of how Jesus is to be apprehended apart from his earthly body.

But however we understand it (and perhaps it is better to scrap the question "how"?), the presence of Jesus is basic to Christ's Supper, then and now. Communion is a meeting – a special meeting – with Jesus.

2. SHARED ELEMENTS OF FOOD AND DRINK

The second criterion for an identification of Communion within the gospels is the specific mention of elements of food and drink taken and shared by Jesus and others. Although Jesus is frequently pictured at table and was regarded as something of a 'bon-viveur' by his critics, we are not afforded full details of the menu on these occasions. We can assume that Jesus dined at some of the best houses, and tasted the full variety of Jewish fare at that time. It is significant that only four elements of food and drink are specifically mentioned and these always with a sense of deliberation. Of these, three have been perpetually used in Christian worship (bread, water and wine) and the fourth (fish) was probably so used by the early Christians and has been used by the Waldensian Christians from the middle ages onwards. We shall see that there is a case for restoring this neglected element on occasions. (The mention of honey is not found in all the Greek manuscripts. It appears in the King James, J. B. Phillips and Good-as-New versions. It may reflect early Christian practice based on a memory of Jesus himself.)

These elements thus become 'Jesus-food' and 'Jesus-drink' in the minds of Christians. The fact that Jesus is not specifically described as 'taking and eating' the Passover lamb, although we know that he regularly did so, is important, for it means there were no attempts to continue the eating of lamb in Christian worship and custom.

We must not, however, fall victim to the finicky literalism and fundamentalism that Jesus spent so much energy opposing throughout his ministry. If people meet together in the name of Jesus and thus in his presence, with the facts of the Good News inspiring their hearts to worship and praise, whatever food and drink they share will be Holy Communion. Those Dutch Catholic priests who in early Vatican II days' liberation were reprimanded by the Vatican for celebrating the Mass with coffee and biscuits may have been irregular or gimmicky, but true to the spirit of Jesus none the less. Much will depend on whether we believe that thoughts of the death of Jesus must override all other thoughts at every communion, in which case the red wine (or red fruit juice), the blood sign, will be missed, if absent.

3. SIGNS

The third criterion is the use of the shared elements of food or drink by Jesus himself or by the gospel writers as signs to impart some truth relative to Jesus himself. The food and drink are used symbolically or sacramentally. Whether the bread and wine at the Last Supper are used by Jesus as visual aids to portray his death, or whether they are perpetual vehicles for the flow of his life to the believer, or any of the other almost innumerable ways of understanding what Jesus was doing, the bread and wine are nothing of themselves but only matter by virtue of the significance provided by Jesus. In every instance in the gospels when Jesus shares food with others there are overtones – the language of parable from Jesus himself or commentary and skilful innuendo by the gospel writer. On each occasion some different aspect of the communion is emphasized and brought out so that our appreciation and joy at our Leader's Table is the less if it is never included.

The idea that hard, scientific fact constitutes the only truth is a popular modern folly. It is shared by the Biblical literalist who believes that to hold events described in the Bible as figurative is to devalue them. The ancients thought otherwise. For them computer exactitude about the facts themselves was of little value. What was important was the interpretation put on events – their spiritual content. They looked for patterns and markers that would speak of the eternal significance beyond what they experienced. The stories of Jesus are told not to provide a diary of day to day happenings but to illustrate the Good News. We do not need a complete list of Jesus's dinner engagements or tape recordings of all the small talk. What we have are carefully selected and related accounts of Jesus having food or drink fellowship on a limited number of specific occasions, so that we can grasp the eternal realities to which these occasions bear witness and which we can, if we will, share in ourselves.

CHAPTER ONE

WATER INTO WINE JOHN 2: 1-11

'…there was a wedding in Cana. The mother of Jesus was there and Jesus and his friends were guests as well. When all the wine had been drunk, Jesus's mother said to him, "They've run out of wine." Jesus said to her, "Stop interfering, woman! It's not the right time for people to find out about me." Nearby there were six stone water jars, the kind used by Jewish people for ceremonial washing, each holding from twenty to thirty gallons. Jesus said to the waiters, "Fill the jars with water. And they filled them right up to the top. Then he said, "Now go back to the well and take what you draw from it to whoever is in charge of the catering." So they did. The supervisor, tasting the water, which had now become wine, not

knowing where it had come from, (though the waiters knew) called across to the bridegroom and said, "Everyone else serves the top quality wine first and the poorer quality after the guests have got drunk. But you've kept the best wine till now." By showing his special qualities in this way in Cana of Galilee Jesus gave the first clue as to who he was. His friends learned to trust him. After this Jesus went on to Nahum Town with his mother and the rest of his family and friends.'

THE story of Jesus turning the water into wine at the wedding in Cana of Galilee is not a favourite for preachers nowadays. It is tricky. Still less would many preachers use the story as an introduction to the celebration of Christ's Supper. Yet all the criteria we have seen to be necessary for a valid communion are there. Jesus is present at the feast and his presence is crucial, as it turns out. Those who share with Jesus in the celebration partake of a drink that Jesus has provided and that he alone can provide. The gospel writer makes it quite clear that we are to understand what has taken place as a 'sign', the first of a series by which Jesus reveals his special character. Even if we have been reading the story as plain history, the writer's comment at the end bids us go back and read it all again.

Jesus is present at the wedding in Cana. He is there as a guest. The fact that mother is listed as a guest before her son may be because it was a family wedding on his mother's side, or may have deeper significance, as we shall see. The chief lesson the Church seems to have drawn from the presence of Jesus at Cana is that he thus hallowed the institution of marriage, and this point was made in the older forms of the marriage service. Among the early Christian communities there was a party that advocated celibacy, and the story of Jesus' presence at Cana was likely used to confound them. (We have no certainty as to whether Jesus was himself married or no. It is foolish to argue from the complete lack of firm evidence either way. The almost universal assumption that Jesus was unmarried rests on grounds other than historical!) However, it is unlikely that Jesus attended the wedding at Cana in order to assure future generations of his approval of marriage. If a member of the family, or a close friend, he would have been expected and attended as a matter of course. The presence of Jesus speaks of his humanity and his natural involvement in everyday life. The special calling of Jesus and his disciples, though it did involve a radical change in priorities, did not call for an opting out of the world in a monastic sense. Weddings and funerals, as seen in the games the children played (Luke 7:32), were the focal events at which communities would be at one, downing tools to join the general rejoicing or mourning. Jesus' schedule of teaching and missionary activity was tight but not so tight as to prevent him from taking time off to play his part in a major event in the life of the community. It is the Church that has turned Jesus into a monkish figure, to be sought after in elaborate ritual or charismatic ecstasy. But Jesus is rarely to be found in the spectacular or way-out. He is someone who belongs to the ordinary and everyday.

We may not climb the heavenly steeps
To bring our Lord Christ down;
In vain we search the lowest deeps,
For him no depths can drown...

But warm, sweet, tender, even yet
A present help is he;
And faith has still its Olivet
And love its Galilee.

(J.G. Whittier)

Christ's Supper, like Jesus its author, must have about it his sympathy with the simple and commonplace. The attempt of the Church, from the best of motives, to dress it up by increasing elaboration of both verbal and ritual elements runs counter to the essence of the communion and at time comes near to destroying it. It is the presence of Jesus, not his remoteness, we are called upon to celebrate. The medium must not contradict the message.

At Cana, the elements involved are two – water and wine. These two elements are present in regular celebrations of Holy Communion today. In places where it is the liturgical custom for members of the congregation to process the elements to the table for offering, water and wine are often brought in separate flasks, later to be mixed. The water enables the wine to go further, as in Cana, and also reduces the alcoholic potency if fermented wine is used. But the water deserves to be considered as an element in its own right. Water is a basic essential for life. As such it is used as a symbol by Jesus. **"Whoever trusts me will have a supply of fresh water inside them."** (John 7:38) Just as on a planet in the solar system scientists look for the presence of water and oxygen as indications that life may be possible, so Nick the theologian is provoked by Jesus into exploring the possibility of similar factors for spiritual birth and eternal life. Thus believers will be reminded by the presence of water at The Jesus Meal of that God-given basis underlying all natural life as we know it, and also they will be reminded of their baptism, a sign of new life.

At Cana, the two elements, water and wine, do not exist side by side, nor do we understand that they are mixed. Rather, one is transformed into the other. We cannot help being sidetracked by the historical/scientific question as to whether Jesus did or could do such a thing. It is a sidetrack because it is not what the story is about and it is not what we are meant to concentrate upon. But our twentieth century minds cannot escape. Much depends on our view of the relationship between the divinity and humanity of Jesus. If his divinity is preserved in such a way that the full power and authority of the creator is there in the man Jesus, then he is able physically to change water into wine. If, on the other hand, it is considered that in Jesus the divinity is, by God's own choosing, limited by his humanity to his own time and place and by what is scientifically possible at that date, then miracles of this type are ruled out. Both views are sincerely held by many Christians. Much heat may be wasted and nothing proved. The other question, equally nagging, is whether, if Jesus could perform such a miracle, he would. According to Matthew, Jesus at the time of his arrest could have called on twelve legions of angels to save him. (26:53) But he had already ruled out such short cuts to success in his period of contemplation in the desert. He refused to turn stones into bread. He rejected ideas of impressing by magic or bribing with food hand-outs. The possibilities of turning water into wine are of the same order. The nature of Jesus was such as to respond with a reflex action to human need, and for him the response was more important than abstract principles. The situation at Cana was embarrassing. Jesus would naturally feel for the young couple whose happiest day was about to be marred. Jesus performs his action with a degree of secrecy, which avoids publicity-stunting. On the other hand the secrecy is not complete – the waiters know. Would Jesus have risked such a wonder-working in a situation that was far from desperate? The guests at the wedding were neither starving nor parched with thirst. Indeed a stage in the proceedings had been reached (frequenters of weddings will understand) when more sobrietous guests would be beginning to call it a day. If one is looking for a rational explanation as to what happened, then perhaps what the guests received from the hand of Jesus was scientifically-speaking still water – an explanation to please teetotallers! Water from the hands of Jesus is the best vintage; a crust from his hands, a banquet. Whatever view is taken of the scientific or theological possibility of turning water into wine, the real miracle is the presence of Jesus, which always transforms the ordinary into the extraordinary. By his touch ordinary people become worth their weight in gold, sons and daughters of God. This, and not a divine conjuring trick, however impressive, is the Good News.

We have inevitably been sidetracked by questions that are irrelevant and incapable of conclusive answer, but cannot be dodged. We now come to what this communion is really about- a sign by which Jesus reveals his special character. The first clue is the row of jars of water used for ritual washing by the orthodox religious. Jesus was not fussy about such customs and was criticised for his laxity by the Strict Set. (Mk7) In a telling symbol, Jesus has the stone jars filled up, then ignores them. Instead he sends the waiters to the well to get a fresh and cool drink. This he offers as the new wine, the symbol of joy and the relaxing of inhibitions. He brings release from the burden of guilt and fretting remorse. As he told the Strict Set, "You don't put new wine into dirty old bottles. You'd ruin the wine that way. You need fresh, clean bottles for new wine!" (Matt.9:17) By implication, what the Strict Set have on offer is out of date, stale and irrelevant. They are incapable of being the bearers of the exciting new gifts from God.

The marriage feast at Cana can be seen as a portrayal of the Banquet of God's New World, or rather, it becomes so ad the account unfolds. What makes it such is the arrival of Jesus. At first, it is Mary, his mother, who is more prominent. Mary, like John the Dipper (Lk 7:28) is a representative of the Old Israel and the Old Covenant. As such she takes precedence over Jesus since her membership precedes his. The words of Jesus to his mother are as sharp as the KJV and RSV translations indicate and should not be blunted as in some of the more recent translations. "What have I to do with thee?" The Old Covenant and the New Covenant are separate and do not mix. Jesus continues, "My hour has not yet come." Or "I'm not seeking to attract attention". When Jesus uses the word 'hour' in John's gospel, it usually refers to the cross, the moment when he draws the attention of the whole of humanity. For this gospel writer, the cross is the point of revelation of Jesus' special character and the breaking down of the barriers that hinder the Gentiles from having friendship with God. (See John 12:23) Nevertheless, as in anticipation of that event, from this moment on in the story, Jesus takes over and his mother recedes into the background. The humble guest becomes the master of ceremonies and the provider of the fare. When at last the steward hails the bridegroom, we can have little doubt that it is Jesus himself we are now to identify with the bridegroom. The actual bridegroom at the Cana wedding can hardly have been concerned with the details of the catering. It is Jesus who replaces the Old Israel, which had provided and continued to provide people with a drink of a sort, but which was poor in comparison with what the bridegroom provides. "You've kept the best wine until now."

The Communion which took place at Cana was a sign of the breaking in of the life of God's New World, bringing gladness and a liberation from old rules and regulations. Such should be the spirit of the table at which Jesus is host.

This spirit should then permeate the life of his continuing community. Alas, Old Covenant and New Covenant have become confused. They have been mistakenly and misleadingly identified with the two parts of our Bibles, instead of being understood as differing and conflicting ways of seeking to relate to God. (See 'Other Temptations of Jesus' for a full discussion of this problem.) What we call 'Old Testament' is best referred to as the 'Hebrew Scriptures'. They are indispensable for Christians, for they contain the thrilling account of the adventures together of God and God's people before the time of Jesus. They also provide the vital background for our understanding of Jesus as a person of his time, in a historical and cultural situation, and in love or conflict with real people. But we are not bound by God's rules for the Jewish people of the Ancient World, nor are we to accept anything in their scriptures as binding on us which conflicts with the revelation of God in Jesus. Only by reference to the scriptures enshrining God's former covenant with Israel can the Church ever sanction a holy war; never by knowing the mind of Jesus. The Ten Commandments are still sometimes read in a liturgical context at Christian celebrations of Communion. They are out of place. This does not mean there is anything wrong with the commandments (though the Church has cheerfully connived at the breach of at least three of them for a long time), but they are simply not the basis of Christian ethics, nor is any set of rules. We are the people of the New Covenant and the new wine; of grace and joy.

DECK YOURSELVES

Deck yourselves with joy and gladness,
Leave the gloomy haunts of sadness;
Come into the daylight's splendour,
There with mirth your praises render;
Come to him whose love unbounded
Has this awesome banquet founded;
Source of life and power and being
Now to us a welcome giving.

Like the sun, our moods you brighten
And our puzzled minds enlighten;
All the senses intermingling,
You set hearts and voices singing.
In your company, our Lover,
Teach us how to love each other;
All in love by you included,
No one by our pride excluded.

Jesus, bread of life, our Saviour,
Here we eat as friends together,
By you to this table guided,
Food you have in love provided.
From this banquet overflowing,
Sign of love beyond all knowing,
Let us catch your party spirit
And your new life truly merit.

After Johann Frank 1618-77 (also translated by Catherine Winkworth 1827-78 *Deck thyself my soul…)*

CHAPTER TWO

THE COMMON CUP. JOHN 4: 4-15

...Jesus left Judea and made his way back north to Galilee. He decided to go through Samaria. He came to a village called Jacob's Well, near the plot of ground Jacob had given his son, Joseph. The well was still there. Jesus was feeling tired after the hard walk, so he sat down by the well.

A Samaritan woman came to get some water, and Jesus said to her, "Give me a drink." (His friends had gone to the village to buy food.) The Samaritan woman said to Jesus, "How can you, a Jew, ask me for a drink? I'm a woman and a Samaritan!" (Jews do not eat or drink with Samaritans.) Jesus said, "If only you knew what

God has on offer and who is saying to you, 'Give me a drink,' ***you*** *would be the one to ask, and I would provide you with a constant supply of water." The woman said to Jesus, "Sir, it's a deep well and you haven't even got a bucket. How are you going to get the constant supply of water you're talking about? Are you greater than Jacob, our ancestor, who gave us this well and drank from it himself, and his family and animals?" Jesus said, "Everyone who drinks water from this well will be thirsty again, but those who drink the water I give them will never be thirsty. The water I give them will turn into a spring of water deep inside them and give life to the full." The woman said, "Sir, give me this water. Then I'll never get thirsty or have to keep coming here to fetch water." Jesus said to her, "Go and get your husband!" The woman answered, "I haven't got a husband." Jesus said, "Quite right you haven't! You've got through five husbands, and the one you're living with now isn't your husband! You never spoke a truer word!" The woman said to Jesus, "Sir, I can tell you're one of God's speakers. Our ancestors worshiped on this mountain, but you Jews say that Jerusalem is the right place to worship." Jesus said, "Friend, believe me, the time is coming when you won't worship the Loving God on this mountain or in Jerusalem. You Samaritans don't really know what you're worshiping; we Jews have a better idea, since we're the ones whose job is to bring healing to the world. But the time's coming, has come in fact, when people seeking to worship the Loving God will worship with sincerity of heart and mind. That's the sort of worshipers God wants. God's Spirit is like the wind, open and free. God's worshipers must be the same." The woman said to Jesus, "I know that God's Chosen is coming. On that day all our questions will be answered." Jesus said, "I am answering your questions* ***now****!"*

Just then Jesus' friends came back and were surprised to find him chatting with a woman, but they did not like to ask "What's the problem?" or "Why are you talking to ***her****?" Then the woman left her water jar and went back to the village. She said to the people there, "Come and meet someone who told me my life-story! Do you think it could be the Chosen One?" They came out from the village and made their way to Jesus.*

THE words 'fellowship' and 'communion' are used variously in our English Bibles to translate the same Greek word **koinonia**. In more recent translations the word 'sharing' is sometimes used. Much of what we understand by our terms 'communion' or 'Holy Communion' is summed up in the idea of fellowship or sharing by which believers share through Jesus in the divine life. Fellowship, as Christians use the word, means the sharing of life to the full, at its deepest level and in all aspects. The Incarnation – God in human flesh and on the world stage, is God's taking the initiative in establishing fellowship with women and men. The Gospel story can be seen as one great act of Communion of God with humankind. Every incident in the unfolding sequence of events in which Jesus makes contact with people, whether the reception be friendly or hostile, can be understood as a celebration of communion in which even the most evil of people are touched by the goodness, love and forgiveness of God. For the purpose of these studies we put the spotlight on those incidents where the fellowship or communion of Jesus is expressed within the context of shared food and drink. They serve, as do our regular celebrations of Holy Communion, to underline realities that pertain over the whole area of our experience. Unless Holy Communion illuminates the rest of life in this way, it is a narrow, mean, petty act of ecclesiastical self-centredness, the religious equivalent of the annual luncheon of an exclusive old boys' club. The Communion in John 4 underlines and illuminates the main features of Jesus' total act of sharing with all people.

Jesus is beside Jacob's Well and the gospel-writer makes us aware of his full humanity. He is tired…he sits down by the well; he is hungry…his friends go off to buy food; most of all he is thirsty…he asks a stranger for a drink. John's Gospel, perhaps more than the other gospels, proclaims Jesus' divinity – the pre-existent 'Word', the Creator of all things, the Way, the Truth, the Life. Yet the same gospel writer is equally anxious to proclaim Jesus' full humanity – the one who shares the happiness of a wedding celebration, who sobs at the graveside of a friend, whose side when pierced produces blood and urine. The one who is in control of the world's destiny and his own, is tired and parched, sweats and pants like any other human being. There is no contradiction here. Theology for two thousand years has been preoccupied with trying to check the twin heresies that deny either the divinity or the humanity of Jesus – trying to concoct formulas that will preserve some kind of balance. A mistaken exercise, since God has chosen to reveal his divine nature through the medium of human flesh. So the divinity and humanity of Jesus are bound up in such a way that to deny one is to deny the other and to reduce one is to reduce the other. The central nature of God is not power, holiness, righteousness or even hearty magnanimity, but love. The more we identify Jesus as the most human of all humans, the more the central nature of God impresses us. The weary figure at the well is the one who is revealed as the eternal "I AM".

And so, if we are to become children of God, sharing God's nature and likeness, we do it not by denying our humanity or frustrating it, but by cultivating it and letting it flower. Pious exercises and self-effacing deeds inspired by abstract moral principles take us away from Jesus not towards him. By letting our natural compassion, tenderness and fellow-feeling flow – by being more truly human – we become more truly like Jesus and thus Godlike.

The element in the communion of John 4 is water. The water is shared – Jesus needs a drink and asks for a drink and the story would not make sense if he didn't get the drink, though his raising the water jar to his lips is not described. But what is startling in the story is the nature of the one who presides as minister at this communion and the chalice used. The minister from whom Jesus gladly receives a cup is a pagan or semi-pagan, a woman, and probably a prostitute. No respectable woman would be seen at the well at that time of day and certainly not unattended. The well may have been her picking up point, indeed there are elements in the story that suggest she assumed Jesus was a customer, mistaking some of his words for doubles-entendres. The gospel writer says that when the disciples returned they "were surprised to find him chatting with a women"- surely an understatement.

As to the chalice, the gospel writer meaningfully comments, 'Jews will not use the same cups and bowls that Samaritans use.' (GNB) A Common Cup – by today's standards unhygienic physically, - by first century standards unhygienic spiritually. Jesus has no objections.

The implications of incidents such as these in the ministry of Jesus have never been fully accepted by the church. How many prostitutes or even ex-prostitutes gather round the table in **your** church? How many members of your church have a prison record? How many are on probation? If these questions shock, it only goes to show how far the Church has managed to turn the gospel on its head. And even if you do have a few people who fall into this 'Sinner with a capital S' category in your church, how would you feel about them becoming church officers? How would you feel about them presiding at the Table?

This should be the greatest cause of anxiety and soul-searching among Christians today. Never mind the talk about growth, which, whatever its advocates say, means chalking up the numbers. Where are the categories of society who were so instinctively drawn to Jesus but who avoid contemporary Christians like the plague?

It should be noticed that Jesus asked the Samaritan woman to share her chalice **before** her acceptance of him as Messiah, which we assume was followed by her repentance. This flies in the face of much evangelical preaching and practice in which repentance is the ticket to salvation-bringing fellowship with Jesus, a ticket that represents only a down payment to be followed by weekly instalments till the convert's dying day. Jesus invited himself to table fellowship at Keith's (Zaccheus) house **before** repentance, and this is the order in God's New World. Had Jesus preached a sermon to Keith, who was precariously perched on the branch of the tree, "Repent of your misdeeds and I'll come to your house", the God Squad would have cried, "Three cheers for Jesus!" As it was they grumbled, "This man has gone as the guest to the home of a sinner." (Lk 19:7) Jesus was proposing to eat and drink with a man who was yet in his sins! Yet most liturgies provide for a confession of sin and an act of repentance before the sharing of Communion, despite the fact that the early Church recited the pattern prayer (which contains the plea for forgiveness) **after** the meal. The Church should beg forgiveness for reversing the order of the divine sacrifice –"Jesus died for us when we were rotten to the core, and that puts God's love in a class of its own!" (Rom 5:8 Good-As-New)

The Church has re-introduced the hygienic regulations of the Old Covenant to ward off the unrespectable types Jesus loved so much.

The gospel writer obviously regards the sharing of the water from Jacob's Well as a pointer to spiritual truth. "The water I give them will turn into a spring of water deep inside them and create life to the full." Probably the words refer to the experience of the Spirit – the indwelling of Jesus, the permanent presence of the life of God within the life of the believer. Some scholars would say that John's Gospel is anti-sacramental in that the experience of the Spirit is set against that of sacred meals as a deeper and more lasting experience. Others, however, would claim it to be the most sacramental of all the gospels and that by means of such examples as the story of the woman of Samaria we are encouraged to see the whole of life as sacramental – each tasting of that which is good and life-giving a direct experience of God – a more profound understanding of the Spirit.

Be that as it may, the Communion in Samaria points to something else other than the experience of the Spirit, which is rather pushed to the background in the story. Jesus and the woman meet together at either side of a water jar – both as needy people. Jesus needs a drink of water, without which he will suffer discomfort and eventually, if the need is not satisfied, be unwell. The woman needs a friend. Her past life is strewn with unsatisfactory and broken relationships. Even now the one she lives with is not her husband and not a friend either, one imagines. Perhaps he is a pimp – one who benefits financially from another's sexual services. Together Jesus and the woman share their experience of human need. In asking for a drink Jesus meets her on equal terms and both are satisfied.

Christians are so inclined to think of themselves as the 'do-gooders', the strong ones who help others in their need. So often representatives of the Church minister from a position of superiority, conveying a spirit of condescension that spoils everything. Jesus did not begin the conversations at the well by saying, "Now what can I do to help you, my dear? What's your problem?" He said, "Give me a drink", and immediately the barriers were down.

So at the Table we come admitting our need. Needs differ. Some are urgent; some are trivial – though no need is trivial to the one who has it. We meet as friends of Jesus, who both shares our need and points to the means of satisfaction – not a private selfish relationship with himself but a drawing closer to one another through him. The woman did not stay alone with Jesus but ran quickly to involve her community.

There can be nothing private or exclusive about Communion. Because we are all needy, we search out and feel for the needs of one another. We meet with Jesus as the woman of Samaria did long ago, expressing and cultivating the common humanity we share with him and her. The jar of water speaks in its sheer simplicity of the unselfconscious, uninhibited fellowship of Jesus with sinners. The joyful answer to our needs now as then is found in him and in one another.

CHAPTER THREE

COMMUNION IN THE CORNFIELD. MARK 2: 23-END

'One Rest Day, Jesus and his friends were going for a walk through the cornfields. As they went along, they began to pluck the ears of corn. The Strict set said to Jesus, "Look what your followers are doing! They're breaking the rules of the Rest Day!" Jesus said, "Haven't you ever read what David did when he and his companions were hungry? David went into the house of God and ate the special bread, which only the clergy are allowed to eat, and he gave some to his friends." Then Jesus said, "The Rest Day was meant to help people relax, not to be a burden. So you see, we even

have to show you how to enjoy the Rest Day. (Good-As-New) *'The Sabbath was made for humankind, and not humankind for the Sabbath, so the Son of Man is Lord even of the Sabbath.'* (vs 27-28 NRSV)

ONE of the problems of going into print in the way of writing a book is that almost from the proud moment the book appears you not only start noticing the printing errors and embarrassing spelling mistakes which have not been noticed by the proof readers who are only human, but also realise there are some important things you have left out. Michael Ball expressed to me his surprise on receiving his copy of this book in its first edition that I had left out one of the 'other communions'. He had heard me preach a sermon on the relevant text. So far from including it among the chapters, I had no recollection of having preached the sermon, which I subsequently located in my files. My filing system is not very efficient. I am grateful for the opportunity to include it in this second edition.

The incident in the cornfields has the essential features for identification as a communion service. Jesus is present. He is God's invitation to celebrate and to feast. His friends eat in his presence. It's spiritual significance is explained by Jesus in response to a protest from the strict set.

Jesus and his friends were having a pleasant afternoon stroll on the Rest Day - the Holy Day, which for them was Saturday. They walked through the cornfields and plucked the ears of corn and munched the grains. I was partly brought up in the country – Devon, and have happy memories of doing what the disciples did, on many a warm Summer's day. It has the same feel about it as the little bowls of nuts or Bombay mix that hosts provide at a party before the main meal. It is difficult for us today to understand how such a simple and innocent action managed to upset the strict set. Only those of my age or older will be able to remember the old Welsh Sunday and how vigorously it was defended. I was brought up in the best of loving Christian homes but was not allowed to play with my toys on Sunday. I was allowed to do a jigsaw puzzle, provided it had a Bible picture. I remember thinking as a lad what a wicked song that was, popular at the time, "Cruising down the river on a Sunday afternoon". Alright, of course, to cruise down the river on any other afternoon, but not on Sunday. The tragedy is that most Christian people have been liberated from that sort of thing, not by reading about Jesus and his friends in the cornfields, but by secular and commercial pressures. Yes, we have been set free not by our religion but by irreligious and anti-religious forces. Likewise, instead of looking at the gospels and taking note of the way Jesus treated women as equals, the Church, kicking and screaming, has had to be taught the lesson by the secular world. I am in a state of constant amazement how little the Church really thinks of Jesus when it comes down to it, and perplexed how few of my fellow Christians notice the sad fact. The Church's bitterest enemies rarely pick up on it either.

How did Jesus deal with his critics in the cornfields? First of all he quoted scripture to justify what he and his friends were doing. Jesus was talking to people who honoured the scriptures or thought they did. What they honoured was words and texts and not the God whose purposes underlined those words and texts. Jesus met them on their own ground. (The first line of defence against fundamentalists is to know your Bible!) "You think you know your Bibles? Have you forgotten what David did? " Jesus thought highly of David – an important clue to the understanding of the human Jesus. Jesus was not called 'Son of David' by his first fans for nothing. Jesus and David had much in common, especially the directness of their relationship with God. The Pharisees spent more time studying Leviticus. They claimed to know their Bibles but, like all Biblical fundamentalists, were selective. You can see them screwing up their faces when Jesus said, "Do you remember what David did? " They were a bit shaky on David. Jesus had to remind them that David had gone with his guerrilla fighters into the Holy of Holies on the Sabbath and ate the communion bread reserved for the priests. Why? Because his men were starving. David had a different understanding of the meaning of the word 'holy' from that of the religious. Holiness did not have to do with fussy rules about temples and special bread and priests and sacred days. Holiness had to do with what God wanted and what God wanted was for people not to be hungry. Jesus took David as his role model in dealing with issues of this kind. What did he and his friends need that Saturday afternoon? They needed to relax. They needed to be out in the fresh air taking gentle exercise. It was not as if they had been neglecting God's work. They were on a mission tour. They had been to the synagogue in the morning. But they needed a break. So with no Nestlés product to tempt them, they nibbled some corn. That to the mind of Jesus was holy. Holiness was the peace and tranquility of a warm summer's afternoon and friends bonding together in a free and easy way. A shared meal was the strongest form of bonding. So the eating of the corn was not incidental; it was central to the experience. Jesus chose an event from the life of David that included the use of the communion bread to make his point. The communion loaves kept David and his men alive. Jesus by his presence blessed the taking, the sharing and the eating of the corns and the sharing of relaxation and friendship. Jesus is the Bread of Life.

The cornfield, by virtue of its ambience -open to sun and air and to the public, stands in contrast to the enclosed shrine and exclusive priesthood David pointedly invaded. In the days of David, the 'House of the Lord' was still a tent. But there came a time in David's spiritual pilgrimage, a moment of weakness, when he contemplated building for God a more permanent house. The one who as a shepherd had discovered and developed his relationship with God out on the hills among the sheep and the wild animals should have known better. The prophet Nathan brought David back to his senses and suggested he think again.

> **'Thus says the Lord...I have not lived in a house since the day I brought up the people of Israel from Egypt....Did I ever speak a word**

> **with any of the tribal elders of Israel ..."Why have you not built me a house of cedar?....I took you from the pasture, from following the sheep to be prince over my people Israel; and I have been with you wherever you went..." '** (2 Sam 7-8 NRSV)

The God of Israel was an al fresco God! Even Solomon, David's son, who built the temple, expressed his doubts:

> **"But will God indeed dwell on the earth? Even heaven and the highest heaven cannot contain you, much less this house that I have built!"** (I Kings 8: 27)

At the trial of Jesus, the worst thing his accusers could think of to establish his guilt were some words of his, used probably on more than one occasion, to the effect that he would destroy the temple and build another in three days. The fact that the witnesses could not agree on the precise words Jesus used suggests they didn't understand what Jesus was talking about. Neither probably did his friends, though Steven, a junior leader in the early Christian community, became the first martyr for understanding too well- **"The Most High does not dwell in houses made with human hands.."** (Acts 7:48)

The implied criticism, by both Jesus and his ancestor David, of a physical temple was not just about bricks and mortar, but about the enclosed and restricted communion that was the inevitable result of a fixed building. David and Jesus advocated and practised a direct, personal relationship with God, to be shared freely with real people out in the real world.

Finally Jesus delivered a knock-out blow. "The Son of Man is Lord of the Sabbath." We must first examine the significance of the mysterious expression, 'The Son of Man'. In the Hebrew scriptures, more often than not, it is simply a synonym for 'humanity', as in Psalm 8 or Ezekiel. In Daniel it means a community – the holy people of God who are to be the citizens of God's Kingdom (Daniel 7:22). Only in apocryphal writings such as the Book of Enoch, does the expression refer to a superman, the coming Messiah. Jesus seems to have used the words sometimes in reference to himself, sometimes in reference to his followers together with himself, and sometimes in the basic sense of humankind. The use of the words 'Son of Man' requires careful study and there cannot be complete certainty about the precise meaning in each context. Jesus may even have deliberately used the words because they were capable of varied interpretation. Certainly he could not be accused of claiming to be Messiah by using the words 'Son of Man'. 'Son of God' was the title for Messiah, a title Jesus avoided using for himself, though it was accorded to him by others.

What did Jesus mean by the expression 'Son of Man' in the cornfield? The Son of Man is Lord of the Sabbath. The Son of Man has license to decide what can be done and what cannot be done on the Rest Day. Who had been eating the corn? Not

Jesus. It was the disciples who had expressed freedom from the rules in this way. So Jesus is saying that members of his community are adults who have the ability to make their own decisions as to their conduct. They do so, of course, in the presence of Jesus and under his influence. The 'Good as New' translation makes this clearer by translating 'Son of Man' in this context as 'we'.

(Jesus used the expression 'Son of Man' in a similar way to his usage in the cornfield in the healing of the Paralytic Man in Nahum town. He said to the man whose guilt for some misdemeanor has caused his illness, "Friend, your wrongdoings have been forgiven!" We assume that the God Squad's murmurings were in response to a claim by Jesus to forgive sins. But Jesus did not say, "I forgive your sins" but pronounced them as already forgiven. The text links this pronouncement with the comment 'when Jesus saw *their* faith', that is the faith of the four friends who had brought the man to Jesus, vandalizing the roof in the process. These were people who had forgiven the man his anti-social behaviour, whatever it was, by their loving acceptance of him and their continued regard for him as their friend. So when Jesus tells the man to get up and go home, which the man does with alacrity and rejoicing, Jesus offers it as the proof that the friends' work of forgiveness has been effective. The Son of Man – loving human beings in this case-can free other human beings of the weight and consequences of their guilt. No wonder the Pharisees nearly exploded. They probably believed that a rabbi or holy man might declare forgiveness of sins in the name of God – the jury was still out as to whether Jesus qualified for either of these titles- but to accord such privilege to any Joe, Ben or Sammy? Outrageous! Mark 2: 1-12.)

In the cornfields, Jesus went beyond beating the Fundamentalists at their favourite game – 'Quote a text'. He didn't need scripture or the example of David to justify what he was doing. As a teacher or guru, he possessed a calm confidence in his authority, enabling him to say, "You have heard it was said in old times...but I say to you." (Matt. 5:21 etc) The strict set accused Jesus and his friends of breaking the Sabbath. Jesus said, "The Sabbath was made for people, not people for the Sabbath". This amounts to a bold contradiction of the Hebrew scriptures, as the Pharisees would probably have realised. The first chapter of the book of Genesis makes it clear that the Sabbath was made for God. God took six days to make the universe, then had a rest on the seventh day. In fact Jesus just didn't accept that account of things at all. When, after the healing of the lame man on the Sabbath day the strict set challenged Jesus, he said "It's not true what you've read about my father not working on the Sabbath Day. My father has never stopped working and I'm working too." (Jn.5) Jesus did not regard the scriptures as the Word of God. John's gospel hands the title 'Word of God' to Jesus from the beginning of all time. This marks the big divide in Christendom today between fundamentalists who take their stand on the Bible (more accurately, on their narrow interpretation of the Bible) and those who take their cue from Jesus, whose yoke is easy and burden light. It is a much more serious divide than the old denominational divisions and cuts across them. Some of the denominations not yet taken over by fundamentalist terrorists – any day now- have made it easy for them by declaring in their doctrinal basis that the Bible is their supreme authority, edging Jesus out. He comes further down the list, looking like an afterthought. The Bible claims no authority for itself. The opening assertion of John's gospel is put another way at the end of Matthew's gospel. Jesus says, "**All** authority is given to **me.**"

Jesus is the 'Word of God'. He also called himself 'Son of Man', 'The Complete Person', and included with himself in the title those who accept the invitation to share his relationship with the Loving God, based not on rules and regulations but on a loving understanding. He shares with his followers freedom to interpret for ourselves what was intended in the gift of the Sabbath, and by implication all the other gifts of grace as well. We have only to exercise our freedom like Jesus, with love in our hearts.

The Rest Day was made for people, not people for the Rest Day. The Welsh Sunday for all its good intentions fell short of Christ's principle. People felt trapped and restricted and burdened. The deacons were watching to see if you came to Chapel once, twice or three times on Sundays, and if you didn't, where were you and what were you up to? The neighbours noticed and disapproved if you hung out your washing. That wasn't what God intended. The 'Good As New' version translates the words of Jesus, "The Rest Day was meant to help people relax, not to be a burden."

The words of Jesus should not just be applied to the keeping of Sunday. Sunday is now almost a non-issue, though relaxation is still very much on the agenda. But the principle declared by Jesus in the cornfield still remains to be applied to every issue that needs to be debated among us. For this we need always and ever to be at one with the mind of Jesus

What about questions of marriage and divorce and living together? Christians persist in thinking like the Pharisees of old, trying to hold down the rules they believe they find in scripture or tradition. They even try to make the teaching of Jesus on the subject into rules. Jesus was concerned and angry at the way people kept the rules and treated one another badly. Jesus realised there are no rules to prevent people from being unkind to one another, only new attitudes of care and respect and sensitivity. A fellow-minister, a friend of mine, had trouble with his marriage. He went to the senior clergyman who had responsibility for his welfare. He was told, "Your first duty as a Christian minister is to uphold the Christian institution of marriage." I was angry when my friend related this to me. I believed, and told him, that his duty as a Christian minister was to seek the long-term happiness and peace of those in his care,- his wife, his children, friends involved- and his own happiness too- a difficult and agonizing set of variables. I have no doubt that the needs of people come before the stability of an institution and I believe this to be the mind of Jesus. The Church has a lot to answer for because it has upheld marriage as an institution instead of thinking about what is best for people. Many people get married who ought not to. That has always been and continues to be the main reason for divorce. If people choose to live together without a legal contract or without making vows in Church because that is what suits them best, we should uphold and support them. We should also offer like support to those who choose traditional marriage. Wherever people love one another we should encourage it. Marriage was made for people not people for marriage.

The Church was made for people, not people for the Church. We get so upset because people make use of us instead of attending regularly, paying their dues and doing their whack. The Church exists to be used. We must trust God to ensure there will be enough enthusiasts in the right place when they are needed. We must stop giving people the impression the Church is some kind of trap.

Baptism was made for people, not people for baptism. If we realise that we would put an end to all the theological hair-splitting about whether people baptized as infants can be baptised as believers! What is necessary for the individual concerned? What do they feel God is calling them to do? Too many people are being pushed spiritually in one direction or another on a path not right for them in order to satisfy ecclesiastical sophistry. Baptism was made for people. We can't have 'pick and mix'!? Why not? God's Restaurant has a set menu and an *'Á la Carte'*, and some very good *'Specials'*.

As I put the finishing touches to this chapter for inclusion in the new edition, some Catholics in the United States are urging their bishops to exclude from communion John Kerry, the Democrat candidate for the Presidency, on the grounds that his views on abortion differ from those of his church. So they are still at it, using Mass as a weapon for keeping people in line! Holy Communion was made for people not people for Holy Communion. Christ's Supper has been used throughout history as a means of control or tyranny. The threat of excommunication even brought kings and emperors to their knees. People are still refused communion in some churches when they are known to be living together. "Let people examine *themselves*" is what Paul said. The sacred meal was intended as an expression of God's friendly invitation to everybody. You may as a free choice eat; you may as a free choice decide not to eat- you will still be loved and accepted by God all the same. Jesus said, "This is for you" not , "You are for *It*."

The Communion in the Cornfield is a communion that trumpets personal freedom. The Son of Man is Lord of the Sabbath. With Jesus as your friend you are in control of your own choices. You are a complete person, an adult, responsible, not hemmed in by anyone or anything. In the words of an old Congregationalist manual,

> **'Come to this table, not because you must but because you may.'**
>
> Independent Press 1936)

COME, CHRISTIAN FRIENDS

Come, Christian friends, there's plenty here for all to do;
God will supply the tools you need and give the know-how too.
With God the weak are strong, the over-cautious dare.
Eagerly venture with a song and gladly burdens share!

Enjoy the Spirit's harvest – patience, joy and peace;
As you express and practice love, it surely will increase;
Loyalty, gentleness and generosity,
Kindness and self-control- all serve to set the closed mind free.

Don't seek the bully's prize or power's security;
Don't sit with those who judge, or spread around guilt's misery;
Join with the victimized and be the outcast's friend;
Then you'll be one with Christ, tired and content at work day's end.

(After Charles Wesley – 'Soldiers of Christ arise' Tune: 'From strength to strength')

OC 4-6.

CHAPTER FOUR

THE COMMUNION THAT WASN'T. LUKE 14: 1-24

'One Rest Day, Jesus was invited to a meal by one of the leading members of the strict set. This gave the strict set an opportunity to watch his behavior closely. As Jesus was going in, he noticed a man with swollen legs, standing by the door. Jesus said to those watching, "Is it against the rules to cure people on the Rest Day? Let's have a clear ruling from you, yes or no?" They wouldn't give Jesus an answer. So Jesus took the man with the bad legs to one side, cured him, and sent him home. Then Jesus said, "If one of your children or one of your animals even, has a serious accident on the Rest Day, do you wait till next day to do anything about it?" They had no answer.

Jesus noticed how the guests were all trying to get the best places. He told them, "When you're invited to a posh meal, don't make straight for the best position where everyone can see you. The one who's given the invitations may have somebody else in mind for that place. She may come to you and say, 'I'm sorry, that place is reserved for a special friend of mine. I wonder if you'd mind moving?' By that time all that's left will be a crowded spot near the door, and you'll look a fool as you make your way there. I recommend you choose that spot near the door when you come in. Then the one who's invited you may come and say, 'Friend, I've reserved somewhere better for you. Come this way.' Then the other guests will be impressed as she shows you to your place. Those who try to make themselves look important only make themselves look silly; those who act with modesty earn respect."

Then Jesus said to the one who had invited him, "Next time you have a party or invite people to a meal, don't invite your family and friends or your rich neighbors. They'll probably invite you back, so you won't really be giving anything away. Instead send out invitations to those who would value a good meal - the poor, the disabled, the lonely, people with special needs. You'll get a good feeling if you're generous when there's nothing in it for you. You should wait till the end of time for your pat on the back." One of the guests said, "That will be a happy day! There'll be plenty to eat for the citizens of God's New World!" In reply, Jesus told this story:

"There was once a man who had plans for a big party. He sent out lots of invitations. When he'd got in all the food and prepared it, he contacted everybody he'd invited, with the message: 'Come and get it- it's all ready!' But they all gave their apologies. One said, 'I've

just bought a new property and I must go and inspect it. I'd love to come to your party. Perhaps another time?' Another one said, 'I've bought some new business equipment and I can't wait to try it out! So sorry!' Another said, 'I'm afraid you've chosen a very inconvenient date. I'll be away on my honeymoon!' These replies upset the man who'd gone to so much trouble. He used an agency to get in touch with all the poor people of the town and invited them to the party. Even so, when all these people had arrived and it was time for the party to begin, there was still plenty of room. So he sent some of his helpers out into the streets and into the country to look for those living rough in shop doorways and under hedges. He said, 'Do your best to get them to come. I'm determined to have a houseful! Those on my original list who turned down my invitation will miss the most exciting event of all time!' " (Luke 14: 1-24)

THE story recounted in Luke 14 is not that of a communion service. It is included in this series because it might have been. Jesus was present at the table; it was the sacred Rest Day; a meal was shared and Jesus used the meal to convey spiritual truths. This is one of the many occasions when Jesus is pictured as an invited guest at a dinner table. "In life no house, no home, my Lord on earth might have..." Jesus, of his own free choice, deliberately made himself dependent on the hospitality of others, whether in the houses of respected pillars of society as in this story, or in the homes of disciples or sympathizers such as that of Rocky's mother-in-law or of Martha, Mary and Larry, or in the homes of social outcasts such as Matthew or Keith (Zaccheus). In this was

Jesus humbly put himself in the debt and at the mercy of other people. Sometimes the invitation and the reception was warm; at other times it was distinctly chilly. (See Luke 7:36-50) Sometimes it would seem that Jesus was invited to a meal out of curiosity or perhaps social one-upship rather than out of any real affection or genuine quest for the truth. Such hosts must have been somewhat taken aback when Jesus made use of the opportunity to criticise their lifestyle. (Luke 11:37ff) The atmosphere on such occasions can hardly have been convivial. The accepting by Jesus and his friends of hospitality from any willing to provide it was also part of his missionary strategy and was the pattern for the seventy-two sent out by Jesus to announce God's New World to the Gentiles. (Luke 10) There is no better way of getting to know someone or enable a sharing of mind and heart than in the relaxed atmosphere of a meal. Jesus could in this way establish and cement contacts and get to know precisely who was with him and who was not and to what degree. There would be an opportunity to explain in greater detail points he had made in his public teachings in the worship centres or the open air and to answer questions. Above all, for those willing to accept it, the shared meal was a parable of God's New World. In sharing food with Jesus, hosts and guests alike have communion with him and share in his special relationship with God. At times this happened (Luke 5:27-35) and at other times it did not, as on the occasion under consideration.

The classlessness of Jesus is something to be wondered at. He could be in the home of an outcast one day and in the home of a member of the respectable upper-crust the next. It is easy to see how this caused problems in the minds of the more respectable hosts because according to the ideas of ritual cleanliness of those times, contamination could be passed along the line. Members of the strict set would not eat with tax collectors. But for the most precise, to eat with someone who had previously eaten with those collaborators with the enemy amounted to the same thing. It was risky having a meal with Jesus – you never knew where he had been! (Especially since he did not always wash his hands!) But what were the feelings of the outcasts when they saw Jesus going in to be wined and dined at some of the posh houses? They might have felt it a kind of betrayal. Jesus was hobnobbing with those who were their oppressors and who looked on them with contempt. Was he playing a double game? They need not have worried. Jesus usually gave the posh a rough ride. However, it is possible for us to react in such a way to the Church's rooted alliance with the establishment that we end up by treating the privileged as a new class of outcasts. Understandable, it is none-the-less a mistake. Jesus was the man for everybody. He ate with the Pharisees, not because they were respectable, but because like the tax collectors and prostitutes, they too were sinners. The 'Friend of Sinners' could not leave out the worst culprits. Those who are called to minister to the wealthy, the privileged, the respectable and the well behaved need our sympathy and our prayers. Theirs is the toughest assignment.

Jesus was present; a meal was shared; Jesus himself introduced the theme of the Wedding Feast, and one of the guests who obviously had heard Jesus before and picked up some of the lingo as well as the usual drift of thought, introduced the idea of the banquet of God's New World. An interesting character this. We would like to know more about him. He is obviously keen, though debatably superficial. He seems to be trying to pour oil on troubled waters. But the atmosphere at the meal table remains tense and embarrassing to the very end of the account we have. There is bitterness in the parting shot, "Those on my original list who turned down my invitation will miss the most exciting event of all time!" As always, Jesus the guest has become Jesus the host. Luke is recounting the story of a communion service that wasn't. We can infer from the teaching Jesus gave from his couch at the table some of the things that went wrong.

In the first place, many of the guests at the table – members of the strict set and experts in the old books – had come in order to find fault. Those who look for faults always find them. The table to which Jesus invites us is not the place for argument or criticism. To quote again from that Congregationalist introduction:

> **'Come not to express an opinion, but to seek a presence and pray for a spirit.'**

The critics objected to a man being cured in the Rest Day. They were correct and proper and wrong. As usual they were devoid of compassion, more concerned about the rule than the person. But the Communion Table has everything to do with compassion. It is God's gracious offer of friendship and help to the needy. The final proof of God's compassion was to be given in his broken body and spilt blood. Those who would receive this compassion must themselves be open to compassion. The compassion of Jesus does not come through many different channels so that we can plug some of them up while we keep our own tap full on. There is only one channel, which is in full flow, and we cannot drink without others drinking at the same time.

Then there was pushing and shoving – proof of lack of humility. Jesus found himself obliged to give a lecture on good manners. The days are past (almost) when the Squire and his family regarded it as their right to come to the table before the farm-hands. In some traditions the president at the table is invariably the first to partake of the elements. Surely Christian manners should incline her or him to be the last? Alas, good manners do not necessarily indicate a corresponding attitude of heart. When someone counters an argument with the words "with respect", it usually means the opposite! It is possible to come to Jesus' table with feelings of superiority. We may not shove our bodies in front of others, but we can shove our hearts in front of others, and if we do, it will not be a true communion, not for us, at any rate!

The 'Closed Communion', which many churches still operate, whether closed to those not signed on as members, or closed to those of other denominations, is an indication of assumed superiority. Some will argue that it is necessary to protect Jesus's table from those who are uncommitted or who do not truly believe, or who do not keep the rules or whatever. Jesus does not wish and does not need to be protected from such people. To exclude anyone who wishes to come to the Table from so doing, amounts to thinking that we are in a different category in relationship to God's grace than they are. The moment we do that, communion ceases.

As Jesus looked round the table, he saw that all the club were there. There were no outsiders, no gate-crashers. "My house this week; your house next week; Jo's the week after." A closed circle was something Jesus could never tolerate. If there is that within a church that discourages certain types of people from feeling at home, especially those who need help and feel they have nothing themselves to offer, then the communion will be in danger of being short-circuited and the power will not get through.

Finally, Jesus told the parable of the excuses. Jesus pointed to the table of his earthly host and spoke of a table laid by a heavenly host, to which all are invited. Much can be said and entertaining sermons contrived on the subject of the excuses. They were rather feeble. The parable is often the text for an evangelical sermon with an appeal, "What's *your* excuse?" Valuable though it may be to confront people with such a challenge, it really misses the whole point of the story in the context in which it is set. It has to do with the spirit in which the invitation of Jesus to come and dine is considered. We suppose that if one had not just bought a new property he might have dragged himself along. What an attitude! "I'll come to your party, God, if I've nothing else on." There is no sense of privilege, no sense of joyous gratitude.

The attitude of the invited guests is meant to be contrasted with the attitude of those who eventually come to the meal. The words, "Compel them to come in" (KJV) are crucial. Anyone seeking for proof of the demonic need look no further than the use of these words by the institutional church as a call to persecute, or to use methods to gain converts that are not consistent with the Good News – emotional blackmail and such-like. In the parable the words reflect an obvious situation. These tramps, these down-and-outs would need some persuading, for they would be reluctant. But their reluctance would be quite unlike that of the others. They do not consider themselves worthy. They will feel out of place with their old clothes and rough manners. This type of reluctance is contrasted with the reluctance of those who think that by presenting themselves at his table they are doing Jesus a favour.

The Christian community should ask itself what precisely it is engaged in doing that will 'compel' the 'outsider' to respond to the invitation of Jesus, in this sense. Is its love and compassion so compelling that the natural barriers of shyness and discomfort will be overcome? Perhaps if the regular Christian were to adopt an attitude more akin to the attitude of vagrants when they realise God's love for them, it would help to create the necessary atmosphere of openness that should distinguish Christ's Table. But please, not by mouthing self-deprecating humbug about being 'unworthy' or even a 'wretch'. God does not look on people as wretches and does not delight when people use that kind of language to describe themselves. I fail to understand the motives of Christian ministers when they oblige people to sing such words, even if the tune is popular!

It is a serious thing to say that in certain circumstances what appears to be a service of Holy Communion is not so. But this is what the story is Luke 14 is saying. Criticism, feelings of superiority, exclusiveness, the grudging spirit – these destroyed the communion at the house of the Pharisee, though Jesus himself was there. We have been warned!

Here is that old Congregational invitation in full:

Come to this sacred Table, not because you must but because you may:
come not to testify that you are righteous,
but that you sincerely love our Lord Jesus Christ, and desire to be his true disciples:
come, not because you are strong, but because you are weak;
not because you have any claim on heaven's rewards,
but because in your frailty and sin you stand in constant need of heaven's mercy and help:
come not to express an opinion,
but to seek a Presence and pray for a Spirit.

(A Manual for Minsisters: Independent Press 1936)

AMAZING GRACE

(Button Polished)

Amazing grace (how sweet the sound!)
That saw the worth in me;
I once was lost, but now am found,
Was blind, but now I see.

When ignorance ruled by fear in me
Then grace my fears removed;
How great that hour of setting free-
To know that I was loved!

'spite accident and foolish choice
I have survived thus far;
God's loving-kindness had a voice
Or I would not be here.

Good things are what Love promised me
And I trust what loves says;
The God of grace my help will be
Now and for all my days.

(After John Newton 1725-1807)

CHAPTER FIVE

BREAD FROM HEAVEN. JOHN 6: 1-15

'Jesus went to the other side of Lake Galilee. He was followed by a lot of people attracted by his success in healing. Jesus went up the mountain and found a place to sit with his friends. It was springtime. When Jesus looked up and saw the size of the crowd making its way toward him, he asked Philip, "Where can we buy enough food for all these people?" (This was a test for Philip. Jesus has already made his plans.) Philip replied, "Six month's wages wouldn't buy one mouthful each!" Another friend, Andrew, Rocky's brother, told Jesus, "There's a youngster here with five loaves of barley bread and two fish. But they won't go very far!" Jesus said, "Get everybody to sit down." There was plenty of grass

to sit on, and about five thousand sat down. Then Jesus took the loaves, said "thank you" to God and passed them round to the people sitting down. He did the same with the fish, and everyone had as much as they wanted. When they had all finished eating, Jesus told his friends, "Go round and pick up the leftovers. We can't have any waste!" So they went round and collected twelve baskets full of scraps from what was left of the five barley loaves. What Jesus had done impressed the people so much, they started to say ,"This is the messenger the world has been waiting for!" As soon as Jesus realized the people were going to force him to become their political leader, he went back up the mountain alone.'

SOME of the communion services of Jesus we have thought about so far may seem to have been a bit point stretching. But there should be no doubt in the case of the feeding of the five thousand. All four gospel-writers tell the story in such a way as to indicate that a communion is taking place. Jesus is present and he is the host. The elements which are shared – bread and fish – are supplied from among the congregation, a feature reflected in the custom in some traditions of the people bringing the elements to the table – possibly the origin of the custom. Each participant in the meal receives Jesus' blessing and the food directly or indirectly from his hands. Also clear from all the accounts is that Jesus intended his guests to learn a lesson from the meal that would be of relevance to their future well being. In both Mark and John the meal is followed by discussions as to the meaning of what had taken place.

There are many little touches that remind us of our communion services. The formal 'taking' of the bread and prayer of thanksgiving, and in Mark the breaking of the bread and orderly distribution by the disciples; (Mark 6: 30-44) such words as 'the same way' applied to the second element; even the gathering of the fragments, reminding us of the concern for the left-overs in some traditions.

The second element is fish. If all the occasions of communion with Jesus are taken together, the fish appears as a more frequent element than wine. Some early portrayals of the eucharist in the catacombs show fish being used as the second element in the place of wine; other pictures show the fish together with the wine. [Fn.1] The epitaph on the tomb-stone of Avircius Marcellus (about 200 C.E.) describes him receiving bread, wine and fish on his visits to the churches of Syria in the steps of Paul. The word used for fish in John 6 and in John 21 where again fish is used for communion, is not the well-known 'Ichus', but the word for a dried or pickled fish usually eaten as a tit-bit with bread. The use of the word may reflect the use of such a convenient morsel in celebrations of communion in the early Church. It would be handy and capable of preservation like the wafer used in Catholic and some Anglican churches. The Christian mission began on the shores of Lake Galilee amongst fisher folk and the fish became one of the most powerful symbols among the early Christian communities, preceding that of the cross. It became a secret sign in a persecuted Church and the letters of the Icthus (Greek for 'fish') formed an acrostic proclaiming Jesus as Saviour. [Fn.2] Today, many who wish to be identified as Christians put the sign of the fish on the back of their car. Since the words of Jesus to Simon and Andrew, "**How would you like to be my friends and fish for people?**", fishing has been a metaphor of the Church's mission. The Salvation Army today refers to its evangelical outreach as "fishing".

Even without the external evidence we have to hand, it is a fair assumption from the gospels alone that fish was used in the communion services of the first Christians. The Waldensian Christians who date from the twelfth century either revived or picked up the tradition, ensuring its survival to the present day. [Fn.3.] There is an intriguing possibility that the tradition of the use of fish was never completely broken. The Waldensian protest against the main body of the Church at the time may have been not so much a call for 'reformation' on the lines of Luther five centuries later, as an attachment to old ways that were being swept aside by the Church's increasing tendency to formalism and remoteness from the people, especially in the conduct of the sacred meal. Fish was not easy to handle in a dignified way. It may have fallen victim to the same attitude of mind that led the clergy to deny the cup to the laity for fear of clumsy handling. In the long term, the almost complete disappearance of the fish from Holy Communion represents the triumph of the Pauline tradition over other traditions including the Johannine- a narrowing of the celebration in both ritual and meaning. It is time to restore the fish to the rightful place in our Christian meals.

As with the communion at Cana in Galilee, we cannot help getting sidetracked on the question of what happened. The first readers of the story would not have been so sidetracked, since being happy with the idea of a supernatural happening they could go straightway to the more important meaning of the happening. It is no good us trying to pretend we can become like them by some kind of primitivization of our minds and feelings. The end product of that exercise is the spiritual zombie. There are, regrettably, a few of those about. The first Christians were only primitive in respect of their lack of scientific knowledge and attendant forms of reasoning. They were not primitive in their ability to see the divine in the human and the wonders of God in the ordinary. Fundamentalist self-emptying of the intellect rids of contemporary knowledge but fails to recapture that of the first century, partly because the skills necessary to understand first century Christianity are jettisoned with twenty-first century knowledge, and more important, because first century Christianity was based on an opening up of the mind and spirit to what ever truth God would send through whatever source of mediation. The Fundamentalist is concerned only to close options.

For me no explanation of what happened in the feeding of the five thousand seems to work, neither literalist or rational. But my twentieth century origins means that my mind insists that there is an explanation, and from that I cannot escape, or the restlessness of it. Here, apologetically, I simply mention the chief options that have been presented so far. Perhaps the truth as yet remains undiscovered. A miracle of creation in which the ruler of land and sea, as symbolized by the bread and fish, demonstrates that rule, as in the calming of the storm? A miracle of sharing in which a lad's generous gesture touches the hearts of others to do the same? A miracle of hunger in which each receives only a token crumb, yet the pangs of hunger cease? Somehow, none of these explanations rings quite true.

The meaning of what took place is what we are meant to concentrate on. The communicants were Jews. It was Passover, a very highly charged time for the Jews, when they remembered God's presence with them in the past. The communion took place in the desert. Moses had led God's people through the desert after the Exodus. The unleavened bread would also remind them of the Exodus. Nostalgia produced a longing, a dissatisfaction, an anxiety to see God's promises fulfilled which, for a moment, seemed to be fulfilled in Jesus. Jesus was hailed as the Prophet, the new Moses, or a new deliverer king like David, or both. And this is where the people went wrong. It was not that they were expecting too much of Jesus. They were expecting too little. Jesus said, **" You're mistaken in thinking in thinking it was Moses who gave you bread from the sky. It's the Loving God who provides you with food."** (v32) The communion was not, like the Passover at that time, a record of past triumphs and the hope of their repetition, but the creating of a new hope, a new hunger that can only be satisfied by the presence of God with the believer, in all completeness – the Bread of Life. God offers not temporary alleviation of physical hunger or of nationalistic frustrations or of anything on the same level. God offers full and complete alleviation of hunger for God. The lesson is that for true satisfaction it is necessary to have the right sort of hunger. Junk food may give a sense of being full up for a time, but for lasting health you must strive for a balanced diet with the right vitamins. This involves not only education, but a re-adjustment of desires. **"Don't waste your energy on food that goes off."** (v.27)

The people who had experienced the communion came back for more. More what? More bread rather than more of Jesus, the Bread of Life. This is the point behind the discussion about Moses and his feeding of the Israelites with manna. Moses had the same problem as Jesus. The people under his leadership also thought in terms of the satisfaction of physical hunger- a matter if life and death for them. But they failed to realize that, in that initial satisfaction, God was offering them a more complete satisfaction. The sacrament of manna fails to work because it is understood as the satisfaction of desire rather than the creation of desire. In Jesus God is present in person. The bread and the fish are the appetizers, not the main course. The Holy Communion becomes idolatry not by some mistaken theology of where precisely the presence of God is to be located, but when its performance and the satisfaction that flows from it becomes the only and final goal. It is like vacating the cinema after the trailer, having taken it for the main film. Jesus feeding the five thousand was not in contradiction to his reply to temptation in the desert, **"People cannot live just on bread,"** (Matt.4:4) but an illustration of that text. His compassion for the starving multitude and his prayer for daily bread precedes the mystical union of the believer with him in terms of temporal necessity. In John's gospel the sermon comes after the meal, not before. And let's be quite clear that what the Christian sacrament creates desire for is not pie in the sky. The full life offered in God embraces the continuing provision of physical needs as well as provision for personal and cultural fulfilment. The desire created is not for the bare material nor for the hazy spiritual, but for life in all its fullness.

Is it possible to change someone's desires? Is it possible, by the taking of the sacrament, to steer the strange and chaotic mixture of cravings which mill around in most of us, in a new direction? The world of business operates on the supposition that desire can be manipulated. Advertising has frequently to do with convincing people they want things for which they have no need. Sometimes an obvious need will produce a product. But very largely our consumer economy is based on a different order: 1) Produce the product 2) Create the desire for it 3) Sell. Trends in the fashion of clothes, for example, begin usually with the fashion designers. The public has then to be persuaded that this is what it wants in various magazines as 'what the well-dressed man will be wearing this summer', and so on. We have to re-adjust our desires to these new fashions because what looks good today somehow looks daft tomorrow. The few who resist this pressure usually catch up two or three years later, perhaps when they buy the cast-offs from the charity shop. The world of pop music provides another illustration. What teenagers enjoy listening to amounts very largely to what they are told other teenagers enjoy listening to, and the rapid changes in the charts are reflected in rapid swings from enchantment to boredom. Along the line some good music is produced and knowledgeable collectors will go on buying 'golden oldies'. But we cannot escape the overall impression that the pop world is first and foremost big business. The aim is to sell, and selling depends on the creation of desire.

Pornography is a more disturbing case in point. Everyone has a sex-drive, but this differs greatly in intensity and in direction from one person to another. For a minority in whom the desire appears to be low, some degree of stimulation may be necessary if they are to find complete fulfilment as persons, though this is a matter of opinion. They may be happier left alone. Desires, like Sleeping Beauty, usually need a gentle awakening. For most Prince Charming or his equivalent fulfils this role. What pornography appears to be doing for most of the time is not ministering to the basic desires but rather seeking to push desire to its limits and to trade upon it. Christians continue to oppose pornography for the wrong reasons. Many, alas, find the display of the naked human body and sexual activity disgusting. Both are God's gifts. What is disgusting is the manipulation of sex for commercial ends without any concern for the consequences in the lives of individuals. Probably it can never be proved whether there is any link between the deliberate inflation of sexual desire and cases of rape or the abuse of children. What we can be sure about is that those who produce and peddle the material are unconcerned either way. Their concern is money, not people.

I have given these examples to illustrate the point that the world of business operates on the assumption that our desires can be changed. Whether it is washing powder, cream cakes or toys for the children at Christmas, the game is the same. Paul also assumed this possibility, influenced by the teachings of Plato as well as by Jesus.

> **"There are plenty of good things in this world for you to appreciate and enjoy. There are many forms of truth, many causes that deserve support, campaigns for justice, societies with a good name, projects that benefit the community. These are the things you ought to be interested in."** (Letter to Philiptown 4:8)

Paul is advocating a manipulation of desire, which we must undertake ourselves, towards that which is good. It is a matter of decision, of stimulating our interests in the right direction. Anyone who has tried to give up smoking or to lose weight knows that success ultimately depends on whether desire has been changed – from the desire for food or a fag to a desire for better health. Unless this shift in desire has first taken place, the exercise will prove a waste of time.

Friends of Jesus make a deliberate choice and set their desire on God's New World. In this shifting of desire the sacrament of Holy Communion plays a vital role. The worshipper, still a battleground of conflicting desires, approaches the table determined to allow the bread, wine and fish to increase, build upon, re-awaken desire for working alongside God and for sharing God's nature.

MAY THE MIND

May the mind of Christ, my saviour
Live in me from day to day,
By his mighty love inspiring
All I do or say.

May his nature govern fully
All my senses, hour by hour,
So that, friend and hostile loving,
Gone is evil's power.

May the peace beyond describing
Stay with me in everything,
calming when I'm called to comfort
Those who cry in pain.

May the joy of Jesus fill me,
To life's venture adding zest,
Talking, laughing, singing, playing,
Bringing out my best.

May I run with zeal towards him;
Walk with him as company;

Sit and listen to his wisdom;
Till he's seen in me.

(After 'May the mind of Christ my Saviour' – Kate Wilkinson)

Fn.1.See *The Early Christian Church Vol.2 Carrington.*
Fn.2. *Celsus 'The true Word'.*
Fn.3. *F.J. Durnbaugh 'The Believers' Church, Herald Press, Scottdale 1985*

CHAPTER SIX

REPEAT PERFORMANCE
MARK 8: 1-10 & 14-21

'It was during his visit to foreign parts that Jesus found himself with a large crowd of hungry people. Jesus called his friends together and said, "I'm concerned about all these people who've been with me for three days and haven't eaten. If I send them away hungry, some may collapse before they get home, because they've come a long way." The friends asked, "How can we get enough bread to feed everyone, out here in the country?" Jesus asked how many loaves there were, and they told him "Seven". Jesus told the crowd to sit down and took the seven loaves. He said "thank you" to God, broke the loaves and gave them to his friends to pass among the crowd. They also had a few small fish. Jesus thanked God for

these and handed them on to be passed around. The crowd had as much to eat as they wanted and seven baskets of leftovers were collected. About four thousand people were fed before being sent home. Then Jesus boarded a boat with his friends and made for the west side of the lake.

(v14) Jesus' friends had forgotten to bring any bread; they only had one loaf in the boat. Jesus said, "Don't buy your bread from the strict set or from Herod's friends" They discussed with one another what Jesus had said, thinking that Jesus was talking about shopping. Jesus overheard them and said, "What's all this talk about bread? Don't you understand yet what I'm getting at? You're not using your eyes or ears! Think back! When I broke the loaves for the five thousand, how many baskets of leftovers did you collect?" They replied, "Twelve." "And what about the seven loaves for the four thousand, how many baskets of leftovers that time?" They replied, "Seven." Jesus said, "You haven't made sense of the clues yet, have you?" '

MARK chapter eight records what may be called the Cinderella Communion – neglected, rarely read and rarely mentioned. Everyone knows the story of the feeding of the five thousand. How many know that Jesus is recorded as feeding four thousand at some later date, and does it matter? The story strikes us as a bit of an anti-climax. Four thousand fed with seven loaves does not seem so much of a miracle as five thousand fed with five loaves. It seems in every way less important. All four gospels record the five thousand; only Mark and Matthew the four thousand. Some scholars think they are alternative recordings of the same occasion on account perhaps of some confusion among the eyewitnesses as to the exact details.

But there is another possibility. The numbers involved on both occasions may have nothing to do with the size of the crowd or the extent of the miracle. They are meant to be understood symbolically, either by Jesus or by the gospel writers. The use of numbers to convey spiritual meanings was commonplace among the Jews and all the ancient peoples. (Jesus' forty days in the desert was almost certainly meant as a reminder of the Israelites' forty years in the desert and, in symbol, the prelude to a new deliverance from slavery.)

We do not know how many times Jesus shared a meal with a large crowd. Probably a certain order and ritual was established on such occasions, if only for the sake of decency and good will. But on two special occasions Jesus was perceived as having used the elements available in a particular number symbolism in order to get a message across. This is strongly suggested by his discussion with the disciples afterwards. "When I broke the loaves among five thousand, how many baskets of leftovers did you collect?" "Twelve" they said,. "And what about the seven loaves for the four thousand, how many baskets of leftovers that time?" They replied, "Seven." Jesus said, "You haven't made sense of the clues yet, have you?"

The way Jesus asks the questions, and the way his friends answer, make it clear that the clue is to be found in the numbers. Perhaps, like the first disciples, we shall guess and guess wrong. A straightforward explanation is that the first feeding of a big crowd was for the Jews; the second for the Gentiles. The number five always reminded the Jews of their five books of the Law; the number two, Moses and Elijah or The Law and the Prophets; the number twelve, the twelve tribes. The number four stood for the four corners of the world or the four winds; seven is the number symbolizing completion as on the seven days of creation. We are reminded of Jesus' words at the table of the Pharisee in the parable of the great banquet, **"I'm determined to have a houseful!"** And on another occasion, **"..great numbers of people from all over the world will be guests at a banquet with our ancestors, Abraham, Isaac, and Jacob in the New World.."** (Matthew 8:11)

There are other hints in the story of the feeding of the four thousand that this was a communion for the Gentiles. The meal is set in Gentile territory. Jesus was on his was through Tyre, Sidon and the district of the Ten Towns (7.73 & 8:1) The words, **"they've come a long way"** may also be symbolic. Those 'at a distance' or 'far off' was a well known way of talking about the Gentiles (Ephesians 2:13). Most cryptic of all is the reference to the 'three days' (8:2) reminding us of the death of Jesus. For in New Testament theology the cross is the point at which the gospel is extended to include the Gentiles. **"When I'm strung up for all to see, I'll attract everyone to me from all over the world."** (John 12:32)

If it is right to interpret the feeding of the four thousand as a communion with and for the Gentiles, then those of us who are not Jewish have made a mistake in plumping for the feeding of the five thousand as our favourite story. The feeding of the four thousand is the story specially recounted to speak to us. It may be significant for adjusting our understanding of the scope of Jesus' ministry. It seems until recently to have been taken for granted by the majority of scholars that the ministry of Jesus was confined to his own people and that the exceptions such as the Centurion, the Syrian woman, the man from Kursa and the Greek visitors to Jerusalem, are exceptions that prove the rule. This view allows that the ministry of Jesus was universal by implication but that the implication was not worked out until the Church recognized the mission of Paul. If Jesus did conduct a fellowship meal with Gentile people in their own territory on a grand scale similar to a previous event with his own people, then Jesus went much further in presenting his Good News to those who were not Jews.

A similar question mark hangs over the approach of Jesus to the Samaritans. According to John 4, Jesus deliberately made his way through Samaria, usually avoided by the Jews. He sent his friends to buy cooked food or prepared by Samaritan hands. He had drink fellowship with a Samaritan woman who became a believer and in turn converted many of the people in the village, and Jesus stayed with them at their request for two days (making three days in all). Yet in Acts the conversion of the Samaritans is described as if it were a new and radical venture. (Acts 8) It may be the overall impression of the gospels as we have understood them until now has been unbalanced in relationship to the preoccupation of Jesus with his own people, which, after all, was where he was obliged to start. But we must not forget that Jesus nearly experienced martyrdom at an early stage in his ministry as a result of mentioning God's acts of grace to non-Jews. (Luke 4: 24-30) Much also depends on the interpretation of the 'outsider' figure in many of the parables. (e.g. Mark 12:9) The son who leaves home may symbolize the outcasts of Israel, tax collectors and prostitutes. But this adventurous lad is also the brother who comes from the far country, a land where they farm pigs. The elder brother may have been intended to represent the sulky élitist Israelite, as well as the unforgiving Pharisee, by Jesus himself. There is no confusion whatever in the parable of the man from Samaria. The 'hated foreigner' in the story is a member of God's New World by virtue of his actions, and that is that.

The concern of Jesus for the 'outsider', whoever she or he might be, was a prime factor in his ministry. They were the lost sheep who are given priority over the ninety-nine in the fold. (Luke 15: 1-7; John 10:16) Since the Gentiles were the outsiders beyond all outsiders, it is difficult to imagine Jesus not wishing to embrace them. Time and the limits of human energy ruled out a worldwide mission. It may be, however, that his visit to Gentile territory was more than just a holiday abroad or a summer school for the disciples. He may have used the opportunity to make one dramatic gesture, which would make clear, to all with their eyes and ears open, where he stood in relationship to the Gentiles. He was their man! If something like this happened, the question remains to what extent the disciples understood or appreciated the gesture. They are frequently portrayed in the gospels as being 'thick' or insensitive, sometimes causing Jesus to lose his patience. (e.g. Matthew 8:17; also 8:33; 9:19; 9:33-4; 9:51-6; 10:13-16) But it may be that failing to undertake a Gentile mission soon after Pentecost was due not so much to ignorance as to disloyalty, more or less conscious. Naturally the accounts would not wish to reveal this. Slowness on the uptake is somewhat less to your discredit than wilful disobedience. But it has always been a problem to imagine any body of people quite so thick as the first friends of Jesus are made out to be, despite being humble fisher folk. There is a less congenial alternative, and that is that the disciples disapproved of certain aspects of Jesus' ministry and persisted in their disapproval despite his Resurrection and acknowledged headship. This would simply mean that they are very like us. Rocky, taught by Jesus to forgive seventy times seven (Matthew 18:22) hardly obeyed the letter or spirit of Jesus's words in dealing with Nye and Sapphire (Acts 5). It is not difficult to imagine that he and others found Jesus's leniency towards miscreants hard to stomach and had no intention of being as soft as their teacher in this respect. There is no equivalent in the ministry of Jesus to the treatment of Nye and Sapphire, Simon the Magician or Slippery Al (Elymas) in Acts! One can compare the deliberate departure from the ideals of Francis of Assisi by those who professed to be his followers, even during his own lifetime. **"Don't you understand yet what I'm getting**

at?" asks Jesus. Yes, Jesus's friends may well have done, but preferred to act dim. **"Don't buy your bread from the strict set.."** that is, "Watch out for the exclusive spirit." **"or from Herod's friends."** "Watch out for the spirit of party and faction." It is unlikely that the Strict Set were the only ones who resented the enthusiasm of Jesus for all kinds of outsiders. Possessiveness is is a common human trait. In Acts the Spirit has her own way of bringing the disciples back into line.

In order to be faithful to the example and teaching of Jesus; in order that God's New World be according to Jesus' pattern and dimensions, with his priorities, the Church must turn itself inside out and present its Good News to the outsider in deed as well as word. It must reinstate the Cinderella Communion for Cinderella people. As long as there is the human race, and as long as the imperfect Christian Church remains, there will always be insiders and outsiders. Those who find themselves to be excluded, despised, shunned, the objects of fear, hatred, disapproval or ridicule, are the prime targets for the Good News and for the Christian community's demonstration of the accepting love of Jesus. Categories of outsider will differ from one age to the next as the taboos and phobias of society go in and out of fashion. Christians must be ever on the look out for subtle shifts that will require them to change their priorities. In the time of Jesus the prime outcasts were the poor (always with us), the sick (especially the lepers), the tax collectors (the unpatriotic), adulterers (if female), prostitutes, women and Gentiles. Today the list includes the poor (especially the unemployable 'shirkers' and homeless 'dossers'), the disabled (especially the mentally impaired), those *held* responsible for the death or injury of others in well publicised accidents (the real culprits often get away with it), those with a criminal record, lager louts, drug addicts, gay people, bisexuals, transsexuals, transvestites (the Church will soon be the only agency left continuing the work of the Nazis in respect of sexual deviants!), those with AIDS or HIV positive, those whose ethnic origin is other than European, Romany people and New Age Travellers. Although large numbers of nearly all these categories exist the length and breadth of our islands, to all intents and purposes they are absent (or invisible) in our churches. Some churches will boast a token one or two. There are individual Christians involved in all these areas who draw strength and inspiration from public worship and Christian community, but in their work they feel isolated and out on a limb, often not able to talk freely of their concern. Far less can they with confidence introduce those for whom they care to the church that yet means so much to them. The list will not always be precisely the same. Some categories of outcast today may be the pampered ones tomorrow, however difficult it may be to imagine now. Once upon a time there was a stigma attached to being a Methodist. There is little sign of it today. Methodists and other 'Nonconformists' have worked their way into the ranks of the respectable to the point where they have forgotten what it feels like to be socially despised. In Wales Welsh speakers until fairly recently were regarded as uncouth barbarians; now they represent, by and large, a cultured strand.

Should the Church in its witness adopt the same tactic as Jesus in taking communion to the four thousand? The danger is ghetto Christianity. Jesus intended his actions as a marker that would inspire his followers in the future. Indeed, in spite of initial reluctance, the Good News was taken to the Gentiles. Ideally there were no ghettos. (Eohesians 2: 14-22) But reading between the lines of Acts and the letters of the first Christians we know that ghetto Christianity was a feature of the Church from the start. (Acts 6:1; Galatians 2:11-) Church Growth enthusiasts at one stage made the apostolic example of failure to measure up to the mind of Jesus in the matter of unity one of the guiding principles for growth. Churches are more 'successful' if membership is made up of people of the same type or social grouping. We have to ask what exactly is 'growing' in such churches. Numbers may be. Understanding of what it means to be a friend of Jesus? Less likely! We have churches for blacks and churches for whites; churches for the rich and successful and churches for the poor and disadvantaged; churches for the cultured and churches for the vulgar; churches for gays and churches for straights; churches for radicals and churches for traditionalists; churches for liberals and churches for fundamentalists! The fact that such divisions suit human nature do not make them any the less a denial of the Good News.

It will not do! In an age that has heard the prayer of Jesus that his people may be one, almost as if it had only been prayed yesterday, it is not sufficient for the tired old denominations to practice ecclesiastical carpentry, devising new bounds for orthodoxy to keep others out rather than welcoming others in. What are we to do? The Salvation Army was founded by William Booth because the regular churches could not or would not accommodate the urban poor; the Metropolitan Community Church has been founded because the regular churches have rejected gays. When Christian pioneers, almost out of despair, feel impelled to step outside the Church's stockade in this kind of way, they are repeating Jesus' communion with the four thousand. But that communion was not a signal for break away. It was a sign to the Christian Church to experiment with a wider and more exciting unity.

He drew a circle that shut me out-
Heretic, rebel, a thing to flout.
But love and I had the wit to win;
We drew a circle that took him in!

Edwin Markham (1852-1940)

COME, LEADER DEAR

Come, Leader dear, and make your home
In every open mind and heart;
We seek your joy and peace to know
And in your New World play our part.

We need imagination's key,

The human touch, the lover's zeal;
Then we the contours of your love
Will know, though tongue can never tell.

Now may the God whose love extends
Beyond the grasp of any mind,
Be known in beauty recognized
In every type of humankind.

(After Isaac Watts 'Come dearest Lord..' v 3 may be used on its own as a parting 'blessing'. Tune 'Come Together')

OC7-9

CHAPTER SEVEN

COMMUNION WITH THE TRAITOR. JOHN 13: 18-30

(Jesus said,) "I know all about the people I've picked. Those words in the old books will come true – 'Someone shared my food, then kicked me.' I'm telling you this now so that when it happens you'll know for sure who I am. Believe me, anyone who accepts one of my people is really accepting me, and anyone who accepts me is accepting the one I represent."

(21) Jesus was clearly upset as he said all this. He went on, "It's just as well I tell you – one of you is going to help my enemies to

capture me." The friends looked anxiously at one another, not sure who Jesus meant. The one Jesus had a special love for was snuggling close to him. Rocky caught his attention and got him to ask Jesus who his was talking about. He leant back and whispered, "Who is it, Leader?" Jesus said, "It's the one I give this piece of bread to when I've dipped it in the sauce." Then Jesus took a piece of bread, dipped it in the sauce and handed it to Judas Simson. As soon as he had taken the bread, Judas allowed his evil thoughts to take over completely. Jesus said, "Don't waste time, get on with it!" No one at the table understood this remark. Some thought, since Judas was in charge of the group's money, Jesus was telling him to get something for the festival, or to give something to someone in need. So Judas, the one who had been given the piece of bread, rushed off. It was pitch black outside.'

THE title 'The other Communions of Jesus' is intended to indicate a series in which the one communion commonly regarded as the only communion Jesus shared with his friends is thereby excluded from consideration. Volumes have been written about that communion, its original nature and its theological significance hotly debated. But we cannot ignore it entirely. In the first place we need to reappraise its significance when we come to realize that instead of being *the* origin of Holy Communion, it is one of a series of occasions that together form the origin. True, the Last Supper has its own special significance in the series, but then so does each other communion. Secondly, we cannot avoid a glimpse at the Last Supper if we are to consider the next occasion on which Jesus is described as having communion in John's Gospel. John's Gospel contains no detailed account of Jesus sharing food with the twelve on the night of his betrayal. If John's Gospel had been the only Christian scripture to survive, then without any doubt we would look to the feeding of the five thousand as the origin of the Jesus Meal. On the betrayal night as describe in John, the friends of Jesus have their feet washed – which some see as the equivalent of the sacrament in John – it took place in the middle of the meal and not as a preparation for it. But there is no description of Jesus sharing the bread or the cup with his followers. The only communion described is that with the traitor. Judas alone is pictured as receiving a morsel from the hand of Jesus. The overriding theme of this communion is treachery, and it is this feature that distinguishes it from the others. The spiritual significance of the communion is summed up in the words of Jesus quoted from Psalm 41 as an introduction to the action – **"Someone shared my food, then kicked me."** This gospel here uses the same words for 'eating' and for 'bread' as are used for eating the bread of life in chapter 6. The more we think about it, the more astounding it seems that the writer chose to exclude the other disciples from this momentous occasion of food sharing and to isolate Judas as the only participant. There is perhaps a parallel in the singling out of Rocky in the foot washing – he brought himself to the fore in consequence of his ironic reluctance to be washed. Rocky is to be the denier as Judas is to be the betrayer. Each gets the spotlight as recipients of Jesus' loving action and each subsequently behaves badly – very badly.

If we move from this account of communion with the betrayer to the accounts of the Last Supper in Mark and Paul, taking with us the impression we have picked up, then we find that although in Mark and Paul all the disciples are involved in the meal, it is yet the traitor who dominates the scene next to Jesus himself. Mark begins his account of the meal, as does Matthew, with the words of Jesus, **"Believe me, one of you eating with me will give me away."** (Mark 14:18) After the meal is over, the scene shifts quickly to Olive Hill where the betrayal takes place. (Luke seems to follow a separate tradition altogether in which cup precedes bread and in which the theme of suffering replaces that of treachery. The references to the betrayal are brief.) Paul begins his account with the words, **"This is what the Leader told me, and what I passed on to you. That very evening when his enemies were told where to find him, Jesus held some bread in his hands and thanked God for it..."** (1st letter to Corinth 11:23). And after the well-known 'words of institution' Paul continues with the words that were always repeated as an integral part of the introduction to communion when I was a boy, in the translation current in those days, **"Whoever, therefore, eats the bread or drinks the cup of the Lord in an unworthy manner will be guilty of profaning the body and blood of the Lord."** This is translated in 'Good As New' as **" So anyone who eats the Leader's bread, or drinks his cup in a way he would not approve of, is wounding him again."** Paul continues with warnings of possible unpleasant consequences to follow. Is it not possible that the three witnesses, John, Mark and Paul, are concerned not so much with providing us with an authentic pattern for the celebration of Holy Communion as uttering a warning about the very worst that can happen – to receive God's goodness in vain? Judas betrays despite the loving appeal of Jesus. The Corinthian Christians act with lack of consideration and courtesy for one another in the midst of what is supposed to be a love-feast. In both cases the body of Jesus is torn apart. The twelve is no longer the twelve. The Church is no longer the Church but a collection of nasty, selfish, heartless individuals. Instead of incorporation there is disintegration, communal and personal. These are sick communions as opposed to other wholesome communions, and the prayer of gospel-writer and letter-writer alike would be that they constitute the exception rather than the norm.

I have hitherto made clear that on the basis of taking together all the communion services recounted in the gospels, only a fully open communion is possible. Any attempt to restrict the list of guests at a meal hosted by Jesus contradicts the host's intention. Those eating and drinking then do so 'in an unworthy manner' and debase, even invalidate, the communion. Those responsible for setting out the open table in the name of Jesus must, at the same time, encourage a sincere communion, warning folk about taking the elements in any other spirit than that of love. This is the test, not whether the ten commandments or any other commandments have been kept or broken, but whether the participant seeks to be united to all other participants in a relationship of love. It is somewhat less likely that the newcomer or the penitent sinner will approach the table in the wrong attitude than institutionalised Christians who take their place at table for granted. Judas was a member of the inner circle – the priesthood, the diaconate, the church council, the bishops' bench, or whatever. The Corinthians were a bunch of one-up charismatic Christians. To such the words of warning must constantly be given. Restricting the table to the chosen few is no guarantee against an unworthy participation, quite the reverse. Holding the communion in the private venue of the Upper Room to perhaps a restricted number of guests did not sift out the traitor but simply heightened the treachery. (It must not be assumed that only the twelve were present. Lack of space and the particular need for secrecy was a limiting factor. It is likely that the householder and his family were there as well as the women who were in constant attendance on Jesus, and of course the 'beloved disciple'. A church in Weymouth has a mural above the altar, depicting the Last Supper. Mary Magdala (Maggie) is portrayed coming in through the door!)

So let us look more closely at the account of the communion of Jesus with Judas. The friends of Jesus were reclining at table. This was the custom at the Passover feast, to indicate a sense of freedom. But the gospel writer wishes to describe a meal that takes place 'the evening **before** the festival' (v.1), and when Judas goes out, the others assume he has gone to buy something for the coming feast. It may well be that Jesus and his friends always shared their meals in this relaxed manner. It was the Roman custom and widely copied. It was also especially associated amongst the Jews with wedding celebrations, so it would be appropriate for the meeting of the Bridegroom and his guests, which was Jesus' favourite description of God's New World. On this occasion the seating arrangements are significant. Reclining to the left of Jesus is his special friend, Larry. (Lazarus- see John 11: 3 & 36), in the position of next to highest honor. This enables him to snuggle close to Jesus and have a private conversation. Next to Larry on the left is Rocky. Rocky's position as second-in-command is not a foregone conclusion – he can only talk privately to Jesus via Larry. But to the right is the place of highest honor. It looks very likely that this place is occupied by Judas, for Jesus is able to give instructions to him that are only half heard and misunderstood by the others. The discreet handing of the morsel to Judas is also more easily accomplished without general observation if Judas is next to Jesus. (Larry is close enough to hear the words and understand them and to observe the action.) May be the disciples were invited in turns to take the place of honor. Luke records a dispute about precedence taking place at this very meal. (Luke 22:24) The touchiness of the disciples on the subject was a recurring problem for Jesus. (See Mark 10: 35-37) This time it looks as if the choice of Judas was deliberate. Let's try to take it in! The feast is for everybody. But this time it is in honor of Judas. So Jesus is putting into practice the ethic Paul was to derive from him. **"If your enemies are hungry, give them something to eat; if they are thirsty, give them a drink. That will give them something to think about!" Don't let evil beat you. Get the better of it by doing good."** (Romans 12: 20 & 21) The way Paul expresses himself suggests tactics – making your enemy feel ashamed, 'heaping coals of fire'. But for Jesus the honor given to Judas is not tactics but an expression of Jesus' nature. Jesus loves Judas, his heart aches for him, the situation is painful for him in the extreme. The traitor is known, his character is known, his intentions are known, and yet all the more he is cherished and honored. The unique nature of the love of Jesus is portrayed here and also his unique goodness. Whereas for us the slights, hurts and bad feelings of others poison our system and make it impossible for us to act towards them with goodwill and purity of intention, nothing puts Jesus off course. We are told, **'He loved the friends he had made in the world and never stopped loving them.'** (v.1) If the principle of good triumphing over evil has any validity at all, it must apply to Judas, for in the crisis of betrayal the greatest good and the greatest evil meet. To say that love was defeated in the Function Room would make a nonsense of the Good News. Judas goes out to betray, but Jesus still loves. The words of Jesus about his choice of friends must be understood in this light. **"I'm not including all of you. I know about the people I've picked."** This does not mean that Jesus had not picked Judas but that he had somehow crept into the disciple band. It means that Jesus knew and understood the character of each of his friends, but his words about humble service did not apply to Judas at this point. There is a deep mystery here. If Jesus knew the sort of person Judas was, from the beginning, why did he choose him? The answer that he was chosen specifically to be the traitor makes the whole passion story far too contrived and dubious from an ethical point of view. The death of Jesus was not suicide with Judas a chosen accomplice and therefore an unwitting victim in a hideous game. Jesus in choosing his disciples seems to have gone for a typical cross section of humanity rather than a selection of the more suitable candidates. This is so far from our practice of selecting people for key positions in the Church that it is difficult for us to comprehend. Hurdles are set up (boards and committees of wise men –mostly men) to eliminate unsuitable candidates for the Christian ministry. Jesus still wants them, they are told, but please will they look for some other avenue of service. But the object of Jesus was to redeem humanity in toto, as it is, not a carefully selected sample. In choosing treacherous people like Judas, unstable people like Rocky, loose women like Maggie, those with money to throw away like Mary Dategrove, bad tempered people like James and John, aptly nicknamed 'Thunder and Lightning', cynical people like Twin, Jesus was asking for trouble. But God's New World was to be established by redeeming the bad, not by excluding them. Judas was chosen by Jesus and Jesus stuck to his choice. According to Matthew, Jesus addressed Judas in the garden as 'Friend' (26:50). There was no dropping of Judas, despite what he was up to.

The fate of Judas is uncertain: there are two conflicting traditions. According to Acts, an unremorseful Judas, still with an eye to profit, turned his reward for treachery into property and subsequently met with a nasty accident. (Acts 2:17-20) According to Matthew Judas repented, gave the money back, then hanged himself. We have no certainty which story is true. If Judas was sorry for his actions and sought to atone through his own death, then we feel that the loving appeal of Jesus in the Upper Room and in the Garden has not been entirely ineffectual. The Church's traditional teaching that suicide is an unforgivable sin is based on a legalistic and un-Christlike approach to morality and on a twisted appraisal of human personality that deems it is possible to deter from such action by fear. Whether Judas took his own life or whether he suffered an accidental death, he passed at that point from the judgement of humankind to the judgement of God – the same God who in Jesus loved him as a friend. Both Matthew and Luke close the file of Judas with a shudder. Jesus in his communion with the traitor makes clear his intention never to close anybody's file. The story of Judas as recounted in the gospels should have led the Church to a different view of suicide from the one it has hitherto been inclined to take. We have become more compassionate, but we are still reluctant to recognize the evidence of God's grace in a suicide. We are likely to label the subject as selfish and fail to appreciate the elements of self-sacrifice that may be there.

Jesus dips a bit of bread into the haroseth, a sauce compounded of dates, raisins and vinegar, used at the Passover, but not exclusively so. He then gives it to Judas. From the point of view of Jesus' special friend this is a secret sign to himself and thence to Rocky (if he passed the message on) as to the identity of the traitor. The disciples were rather good at misunderstanding the actions of Jesus and it is possible they misunderstood this one. From the point of view of Judas the incident must have had an entirely different feel about it. He, the honored guest, was being singled out for a special act of communion with Jesus. The sweet and sour sauce that coated the bread seems appropriate to a communion that combined the love of Jesus and the duplicity of Judas. What was the reaction of Judas? Was he touched? Did he hesitate to take the bread? Did he for one moment contemplate changing his plans? The gospel account seems to suggest a hasty hardening of the heart. ' **As soon as he had taken the bread, Judas allowed his evil thoughts to take over completely.'** Yet this quick hardening of the heart is suspicious. He dare not linger lest he weaken. (For those who believe in a personal devil it suggests that Satan realised that if he didn't move swiftly he would lose his prey.) The same formula is repeated with a slight change at the end of the account. **'..Judas, the one who had been given the piece of bread, rushed off. It was pitch black outside.'** At the moment of communion there is an opening chink of light, then darkness descends. Jesus seems to hurry him on. **"Don't waste time, get on with it!"** This is in line with the practice of Jesus on many occasions of forcing a decision either for or against him. Jesus has more respect for the person who decisively rejects him than for the one who vacillates or wants to have it both ways. In the presence of Jesus we come face to face with options we would sooner avoid and aspects of our character we prefer to mask. We do horrible things and cunningly shield ourselves from the horror of what we are doing. Jesus does not allow this. If we are to be cruel in his company it will be with an awareness of the full impact of our cruelty.

Whatever made Judas do it? Materialistic greed? Some find that incredible, but as bad and worse is being done for the sake of money every day. Envy of the other disciples or jealousy that he could not possess Jesus for himself? Disillusionment and loss of faith leading to bitterness and resentment? A failure of courage – switching to the winning side? Differences with Jesus over the party manifesto? These are guesses that have been made, the first one very early on. None of them may be true. Perhaps Judas was ill – schizophrenic perhaps. The point about any one of these explanations is that they are not unusual or shocking from the viewpoint of human experience. This sort of thing is happening all the time. So when Mark describes the same scene, the dipped bread is handed not to Judas alone but to each of the twelve. **"I'm talking about one of my twelve closest friends – someone dipping bread in the same bowl with me!"** Each of them protested, **"It can't be me!"** Each one is obliged to contemplate the possibility they might be the traitor, and each one, not just Judas, shares the traitor's communion. Thus the readers of Mark's gospel, including some of the twelve still living or their friends or disciples, were invited not to gloat over the behaviour of Judas but to accept that for them it had been a near miss. This extension of the possibility of treachery to the others is not altogether absent from the account in John's gospel. When Jesus said, **"one of you is going to help my enemies to capture me,"** the disciples **'looked anxiously at one another, not sure who Jesus meant.'** It could have been any one of them!

The Communion with the Traitor teaches us how precarious is our loyalty to Jesus. Love of material gain, envy, bitterness, cowardice, divisiveness – the things we regard as possibly attributable to Judas, are over our doorstep. The Communion with the traitor also teaches us, more graphically than any of the other communions, that in spite of all this there is a love that will never let us go, a love that calls the traitor 'Friend' and offers the bread of life.

ONE THERE IS

One there is above all others,
Well deserves the name of friend.
His is love beyond a mother's,
Costly, free and knows no end:
Those who once his kindness prove,
Find it everlasting love.

Which of all our friends to save us
Could, or would, have shed their blood?
On the cross he died to have us
Friends of his and friends of God.
This was boundless love indeed!
Jesus is the friend we need.

When he lived on earth rejected,
'Friend of outcasts' was his name;
Now above all praise exalted,
To the title he lays claim:
Ever calls them his best friends,
And to all their needs attends.

Could we bear from one another
What he daily bears from us?
Yet this glorious friend and brother
Loves us though we treat him thus;
Though for good we render ill,
Calls us sisters, brothers still.

O for grace our hearts to soften!
Teach us, Leader, how to love.
We, for shame! forget too often
What a friend you always prove;
But when home we all are brought,
We will love you as we ought. (After John Newton)

CHAPTER EIGHT

COMMUNION ON THE CROSS

THE Christian Church is divided on the question of whether it is appropriate to celebrate Communion on Good Friday. In the Catholic and Anglican traditions it is thought inappropriate. On the black day when Jesus died, communion between heaven and earth was broken. Hence the custom of the Anti-Communion in which the vessels and paraphernalia regularly used for communion are displayed on the bare altar, without their contents. The cry of dereliction, (**'My God, why have you left me?**), interpreted by some Christians as betokening God the Father's rejection of his Son, the sin-bearer, is paralleled by a breakdown in the means of grace for all humanity. Protestant fundamentalists are also keen on this idea, though not necessarily on its ritual application to the denial of communion on Good Friday. Texts from the Hebrew scriptures, aborted from their context, are adduced to assure us that God is incapable of 'looking on sin'. God's holiness consists of squeamishness raised to the nth degree. They do not see that the logic of this assertion is a denial of the special entry into the world of God in Jesus, to say nothing of the ancient teaching that God is all knowing and everywhere present. The God who was in Jesus making peace with the world went wherever sin was (and it was everywhere) and stared it in the face. The holiness of Jesus had nothing to do with squeamishness and in this he differed dramatically from the strict set, the Pharisees. Neither will the schizophrenic deity portrayed in some revivalist preaching of a haughty, ill tempered, intolerant God the Father, poles apart from a self effacing, merciful and sympathetic God the Son, satisfy intelligence or spiritual sensitivity.

Another stream of Christianity seems to take it for granted that of all days Good Friday is the most appropriate to celebrate Communion. The thinking behind such a view is simple and straightforward. The meal is first and foremost a remembrance of the death of Jesus. On what day is it more appropriate to remember his death than on Good Friday? The practice of celebrating communion on Good Friday is continued by many in the Free Church tradition, particularly those who have not been greatly influenced by the cross fertilization from the Catholic tradition in recent years via the Liturgical Movement. Some will only celebrate the meal once a year and that on Good Friday!

There may be a parallel to this division of practice in the gospels. The 'Last Supper' in Mark, Mathew and Luke seems to have taken place in the context of the Passover meal on the day equivalent to our Thursday of Holy Week. John's gospel does not describe a communion on that day, except the communion with the traitor. The author does, however, associate Good Friday with the celebration of the Passover (18:29; 19:14; 19:31), and recounts, as we shall see, the victory communion on that day. Most scholars perceive that this gospel views the cross and resurrection of Jesus, and indeed the gift of God's Spirit, as one healing event, whereas the other gospel writers separate out the events in such a way as to highlight the dramatic reversal of fortune. It does seem that these three gospels are more likely to be in line with the experience of most of those involved at the time, whereas John's gospel embodies a deeper reflection from an observer who perhaps stood somewhat apart. That the significance of some of the happenings on the first Good Friday were not perceived by all observers at the time does not mean that the significance was not there and observed, nor that it was a later pious fabrication.

The story of the crucifixion contains three incidents that are of significance for our study. They may be referred to as 'The communion Jesus refused', 'The communion that was a mockery', and 'The communion of fulfilment'.

THE COMMUNION JESUS REFUSED. MARK 15:21-27.

'The soldiers forced someone to help carry Jesus' cross. He was an African called Simon (the father of Alex and Rufus). He just happened to be passing that way, coming into the city from the country. They took Jesus as far as Skull Hill. They tried to get him to take a painkiller, but he refused it. Then they fastened Jesus to the cross and put it in place. They shared out his clothes, throwing dice for each item.'

Crucifixion is one of the most horrible deaths we humans have ever devised. Yet what strange creatures we are. We also devise a means of relieving the pain. It was the custom to offer drugs to the crucified. These drugs rendered the victims half oblivious to what was happening and were good painkillers. A hefty dose of myrrh mixed with strong wine was probably quite effective. Today we organize vast money-making jamborees for the relief of famine stricken areas. These events are highly publicized by the media, with the stars of popular entertainment well to the fore. We run marathons, we wear red noses, we compete in ingenious and bizarre ways to gain sponsorship (someone spent five days in a bath of porridge) – all very noble and credit worthy. But all this is only necessary because we in the materially privileged countries are largely responsible for perpetuating need in the poorer countries by our greed, over indulgence and unjust trade system. Many of the people who work for Samaritans and similar agencies come from very cosy backgrounds. All honour to them, they have a conscience;

they have compassion; they want to help. Yet the same people often lend their support to the continuance of a social and economic system that will make sure the phones continue to buzz. We crucify, then rush to relieve the pain! The Roman army was one of the most ruthless and brutal killing machines in human history. But it looked after its own wounded superbly with anaesthetics, antiseptics and surgical skill. Our present western Christian civilization did not catch up until well into the twentieth century. Drugged wine was available on Skull Hill. Jesus was offered it, but shut his lips tight as soon as he realized what it was. He refused communion. Why? Maybe the answer is to be found in the Book of Proverbs (31:4-7)

> **'It is not for rulers to drink wine, or for those who govern to crave strong liquor. If they drink, they will forget rights and customs and twist the law against all who are defenceless.**
>
> **Give strong drink to the despairing and wine to the embittered of heart; let them drink and forget their poverty and remember their trouble no more.'** (REB alt)

Drink and drugs often serve as a way out for those who are not prepared to face realities or who wish to abdicate their responsibilities. As one who was dependent on valium for fourteen years and still remember what it was like to operate on one cylinder, I am not shouting advice from the touch line. Sometimes life strikes us as unbearable and the choice seems stark, either to ease the pain by whatever means lies at hand or to pack it in. There is usually a third alternative, but this often takes a while to work out. Inasmuch as prescribed drugs have staved off total collapse and provided a breathing space for many of life's victims, they may be regarded as God-given. We cannot blame victims of crucifixion for accepting their myrrh-laced drink avidly and with relief. But Jesus intended to remain in full possession of his senses. He had set himself to share our sufferings to the full and he was not going to dodge the pain. The world was depending on him for health and wholeness. There was to be no abdication of responsibility. How could he have spoken the words of hope to the convicted criminal at his side if he had been blotto? How could he have forgiven his torturers? People sometimes turn to drink and drugs out of boredom or frustration. Jesus was not frustrated. He was fulfilling his life's mission.

Recent years have witnessed an explosion of interest in healthy living. We are learning, with the assistance of science, what foods and what activities are good or bad for us, though it is not always so easy to change our habits accordingly. Christians should take on board and bear witness to all truth that makes for wholeness of mind and body. That was the strength of the Temperance Movement, despite its intolerance and tendency to tunnel vision. Without being fanatical, legalistic or censorious, we should yearn to be our best so that we can do our best. That should not exclude our personal quest for happiness and fulfilment, for unless we reach a point of ease and good humour within ourselves, how can we bring peace and joy to others?

THE COMMUNION THAT WAS A MOCKERY

'The ordinary people standing by watched in silence. But the leaders tried to make fun of Jesus, shouting things like, "He was good at helping other people. If he's God's chosen leader, let's see him help himself!" The soldiers made fun of him too. They paraded in front of him and offered him some of the free wine they got for doing the job. They said, "If you're the leader of the Jews, where's your rescue party?" (Luke 23: 35-47)

There was a time when children used to sing in response to harsh words or name calling, "sticks and stones will break my bones, but words will never hurt me" – sheer bravado, for nothing is further from the truth. Words can be used to inflict deep wounds and the history of human cruelty can be recorded as much by its words as its actions. For Jesus to have been allowed to suffer in silence would have been considerably less painful without what he had to endure from the taunts of the onlookers, - every cry a nail, every word a thorn! The rulers who had so often been silenced by Jesus with a word, now had their own back, in a spirit of vengeance. The soldiers, who probably did not know what it was all about, were less vindictive. They led a dull, brutish life and this seemed the opportunity for a bit of sport, and they had probably been drinking anyway. The game was 'Worship the King.' The description of the soldiers 'coming forward' suggests play-acting as if in a royal court. It was one of the most highly prized privileges to be the one chosen to offer the king a drink. We can imagine them parading up with their wine bottles, tantalizingly offering drink to the parched sufferer, and then perhaps throwing it in his face or drinking it themselves. A mock communion! The pictures of soldiers of the western allies 'having fun' with prisoners in the 2004 war in Iraq are a sickening reminder that, after two thousand years, soldiering has not yet cleaned up its act.

Jesus was full of fun and enjoyed a joke, even at someone's expense if no hurt was intended. **"We'd miss you like a sore thumb, Holy Joes, humbugs! ...A fly falls into your drink and you delicately pick it out. Then you shut your eyes and gulp down a camel!"** (Matthew 23;24) Indeed, much of Jesus' teaching has been misunderstood and misappropriated because his followers have not shared his sense of humour. They have not accounted for the twinkle in the eye and the chuckle in the voice. **"If your eye offends you, pluck it out"** is not an invitation to sadomasochism. Jesus is trying to get us to laugh at ourselves, in particular the stupidity of our Pharisee obsession with our little sins.

Yet we can be confident that Jesus would have no time for that brand of humour which makes fun of human suffering and weakness. According to him, people who use abusive language calculated to demean or humiliate are heading for the city rubbish dump where they belong. (Matthew 5:22) Some comedians manage to get laughs by acting the drunk, by caricaturing a gay person or by racialist or sexist jokes calculated to depress further those who are already depressed and struggling to maintain human dignity. Then on come the opponents of 'political correctness' who do not like to have their licence to be insensitive and unkind taken away from them. When people are self-confident, especially if they are over confident, then a laugh at their expense can be a useful form of criticism that they should be able to take in good part. But those who are already bruised and battered by discrimination or hostile social attitudes should be spared that kind of treatment. Christians should be sensitive to the reality that humour can be a very effective form of persecution. There are some jokes Christians cannot laugh at and some that they will not find funny. Jesus went all the way in sharing our basic humanity. But there are things he cannot share. He will not gang up with the playground bully. He demonstrates on the cross his choice to suffer with the weak at the hands of the bully. That must also be our choice.

Teach us delight in simple things
And mirth that has no bitter springs.
(Rudyard Kipling)

THE COMMUNION OF FULFILMENT

'At twelve o'clock it became very dark everywhere until three in the afternoon. At about three o'clock Jesus shouted out in Hebrew, "My God, my God, why have you left me?" The Hebrew for "My God" sounds something like Elijah, so some of the onlookers said, "He's calling for Elijah!" Someone ran and filled a sponge with some cheap wine, put it on a stick and held it up for Jesus to drink. Some said, "If we hang around long enough, we may get to see

Elijah, if he comes to save him!" Then Jesus gave a loud cry and died.' (Matthew 27: 45-49)

'By this time Jesus realized he was dying. He said, "I need a drink." This too reminds us of words in the old books. The soldiers went to their jar of cheap wine, soaked a sponge in it, put it on a stick and lifted it to his mouth. As soon as Jesus had drunk the wine, he said, "It's all over!" His head fell and he stopped breathing.' (John 19: 28-39)

Finally comes the true Good Friday Communion. According to John's Gospel Jesus asks for a drink. According to Matthew, Mark and John, a bystander, probably a soldier, gives him a drink. Thus two things remind us of the communion Jesus had with the Samaritan woman – Jesus asks for a drink, and he shares a common cup with outsiders. This drink was given in a different spirit from the drink previously offered in mockery. It was an act of spontaneous compassion. One of the soldiers, at least, had a heart. Jesus: a compassionate soldier sharing his drink: we are two thirds of the way towards a genuine communion. The gospel writers are aware that the third factor is also present – the spiritual dimension. The words of Jesus "I need a drink", remind us of 'words in the old books'. His taking a drink at this point is a deliberate, symbolic act, especially in view of his recent refusal to drink the drugged wine. The scripture is probably Psalm 69 – **'They gave me vinegar to drink when I was thirsty'**, that is sour wine, 'posca', the common drink of labourers and soldiers. The clergy present, had they been willing to think about it, would have got the message. Prophesies concerning God's Chosen (the 'Messiah') were being fulfilled. In spite of their sarcasm, Jesus had not been shifted from his belief in his destiny. He had not renounced his claim.

There was also a message for the friends of Jesus when they got to hear of it. In the function room at supper Jesus had said, "Believe me, I won't drink wine again until I drink it in God's New World!" (Mark 14:25). It is possible that this 'vow of abstinence' marked the beginning of a drink strike, in which case we may have a clue as to why Jesus died more quickly than expected. He was suffering from dehydration. But at the very moment of his death Jesus cries, "I need a drink!" He takes the drink and shouts triumphantly, "It's all over!" "We've made it!" He may now drink because God's New World has come. All the powers of evil, all the efforts of hatred, have been outwitted in a decisive event. John's Gospel sees the death of Jesus on the cross as the moment that marks his victory. The drink is placed on hyssop, the bitter herb taken by the Jews at Passover as part of their celebration of the Exodus. A new deliverance has come, like that of Israel, through bitterness and suffering. Communion is celebrated at the cross. It is all the more striking set against the backcloth of the two false preludes – the mock communion and the refused communion, which between them speak of the twin nature of human wickedness, commission and omission, wilful cruelty and cowardly abdication of responsibility.

CHAPTER NINE

EYE OPENER

'...two friends of Jesus were on their way to Emmatown, a few miles from Jerusalem. They were discussing the events of the weekend. As they were talking, Jesus met up with them, going the same way. They didn't recognize him in the failing light. Jesus said, "You were deep in conversation as you were walking along. What were you talking about?" They hesitated for a moment and their faces were sad. Then one of them called Clover said, "You must be the only visitor to Jerusalem who doesn't know what's been happening the past few days!" Jesus said, "What do you mean?" They said, "Haven't you heard of Jesus from Nazareth, a great speaker from God, who did wonderful things which were seen by everybody? Our clergy and politicians handed him over to the

Romans to be tried and executed. We hoped he was going to be our national liberator. All this happened three days ago now. But some women we know have come up with a very surprising story. They visited the grave early this morning and found that the body was gone. They came back and told us they had seen messengers from God who said that Jesus was alive. Then some friends of ours went to the grave and found it was indeed empty, but they saw no sign of Jesus."

Then Jesus said, "How could you be so dim? How long is it going to be before you piece together the clues in the old books? Don't you know the passages which speak about the way God's Chosen would suffer before becoming famous?" Then Jesus began to explain how the words of Moses, and all the other speakers from God in days gone by, pointed to himself.

As they came near to the village, Jesus walked on, as if he intended to continue his journey. But the two would not hear of it. They insisted, "You must stay at our place. It's nearly night; there's no light left for travelling." Jesus accepted the invitation. When they were having supper, Jesus took a piece of bread, said "thankyou" to God, broke it and handed it to them. At that moment they realized who he was. Then he left them. They talked to one another about it and said, "What a wonderful experience that was! How he cheered us up on that walk together! We understood the old books for the first time!" They went out again straightaway and walked back to Jerusalem. They found a gathering of all the close friends of Jesus. The two were told, "It's true, the Leader's come back to life. Rocky's seen him!" Then they told the others how they had met Jesus on the road, and how they had recognized him when he broke the bread.'
(Luke 24: 13-35)

THE return to life of Jesus was the keynote of the earliest proclamations of the Gospel. For the first disciples the immediate piece of good news was that their friend had triumphed over death and that despair had been turned into hope. This good news emotionally and psychologically preceded the preaching of the cross as the means of reconciliation and forgiveness, for a reappraisal of what had been experienced as a tragedy could only emerge after a period of reflection in the light of the Resurrection. It is probably not fair to attribute entirely to Paul a shift in the balance of the Christian message from the rising of Jesus to his death, especially in view of Paul's first letter to Corinth chapter fifteen and much else besides. It seems to have come progressively in western Christendom as the initial excitement and joy of the disciples gradually faded and the Church became more and more obsessed with the dark and depressing aspects of life. This has been reflected in a change in the character and atmosphere of Communion from a joyful celebration to a solemn memorial; from a victory beanfeast to a gathering around the cenotaph. This shift in emphasis has had as its accompaniment a wilful ignoring or a taking lightly of the evidence that Jesus celebrated communion with his disciples after his Resurrection. Yet this was part of apostolic preaching. In his sermon to Neil (Cornelius) Rocky linked the Resurrection and the celebration of Christ's Supper. "We actually ate and drank with Jesus, after he returned to life." (Acts 10:41)

The sections of the gospels dealing with the appearances of the risen Jesus are tantalizingly brief and sketchy. Yet within them are contained three accounts of the celebration of Communion. Indeed, a new focus is achieved on the accounts if we take these celebrations as the central climax, in each case, of the meetings of Jesus with his friends.

The first communion of the Resurrection, according to the records, took place on the first Easter Day at the village of Emmatown (Emmaus), possibly four miles north of Jerusalem, rather than the seven miles given in the Greek (7 is a symbolic holy number). This would have been somewhere near the old shrine of Bethel where heaven had been opened for Jacob, the ancestor of the Jewish people. Thought of from the point of view of a communion, the Emmatown story has several strange features. The first two communicants of Easter Day did not belong among the eleven 'apostles' who had to wait until later. It may be that the 'twelve' had a more significant status in their own eyes than in the eyes of Jesus. It would seem that Jesus was in no hurry to assure the twelve minus one of his rising. We do not know what time of day it was when Jesus appeared to Rocky (1 Corinth 15:5) but the impression we get is that it was late in the day. The Emmatown folk had not yet heard about it and they had been in Jerusalem presumably until late afternoon. They had, however, heard the reports of the women and the reports of the investigation of the empty tomb. The unpalatable fact for the eleven was that Jesus did not regard them as number one priority. The women, especially Maggie (Mary of Magdala) came first, perhaps in token of their faithfulness at the cross (the true apostles), followed by the Emmatown couple who, as far as we can tell, had no special claims at all. To have to wait their turn for communion is a salutary reminder to the presumed leaders of the Christian community of Jesus' reversal of worldly precedence. The leaders of the Church are to be servants who humbly serve others first, then patiently wait themselves to be served. The custom of the officiant serving himself or herself with the elements of Communion before the rest is not only bad manners but unscriptural and not at all like Jesus. At Emmatown, as elsewhere, when Jesus celebrates he is described as distributing food to others but there is no hint that he first served himself. He is the perfect host. This indicates also the reversal of worldly economics in God's New World. On the whole the Church parallels the 'trickle down' method of distributing its goods, as exemplified by Margaret Thatcher. Grace begins with priests and ministers who pass it down to church members who pass it on to their less committed families and friends and others on the fringe of the church fellowship, and then finally (perhaps) some of it gets to where it is really needed, to the 'under-classes'. The Church has never really taken seriously the cardinal principle of God's New World as spelt out by Jesus, **'The first shall be last and the last shall be first.'** (See Mark 10:31; Matthew 20:1-16 & Luke 13:30) Jesus began on the day of his rising as he wished his followers to continue, driving home his new scale of priorities.

Next, the number of communicants at the first Easter communion strikes us as strange. It is the minimum number normally required for a valid communion – two. This is a far cry from the practice of some churches in pressing for a maximum attendance at communion on Easter Day for the purpose of assessing the number of supposedly practising

Christians for the parish records. A far cry also from the triumphalist communions papal-style where the Church attempts to impress the media with its virility. In Nonconformist piety the words of Jesus, assuring that where two or three are gathered in his name he would be there among them, are frequently used as a message of comfort in the event of a disappointing attendance. (Matthew 18:20) That Jesus chose to spend a few hours of his first day out of the tomb to keep company with just two people, whilst Church and world were kept waiting for the Good News, demonstrates his complete freedom from our obsession with numbers as well as a very laid-back attitude to time.

The first Easter communion takes place in a home. It takes place in a situation of the familiar and the congenial. The presence of Jesus does not invade, but gently dovetails into the normalities of life. There had been no warning of the need to provide hospitality, so the guest would have to accept things as they were. The Emmatown communion is a perfect example of what true communion always should be- sharing with Jesus the commonplace things of life. Not even the earth-shattering event of the Resurrection can displace the value of simple human contacts and conventions. It is the combination of the excitement of the Resurrection with the essential homeliness and normality of the Emmatown setting that largely accounts for the attractiveness of the story so beautifully told by Luke.

Who were these two? Luke tells us that one of them was called 'Cleopas' (Good as New 'Clover'), which may be meant as a clue. John's gospel tells us that one of the bewildering number of Marys at the cross was Mary (Good as New 'Miriam') sister of Mary the mother of Jesus and wife of 'Clopas'. So it is at least possible that the two on the road were husband and wife, Clover and Miriam, uncle and aunt of Jesus. It may be that not all the members of Jesus' family were as unsympathetic to his calling as his mother and brothers seem to have been prior to the Resurrection. (See Mark 3: 21 & 31-35) It is not unknown for youngsters who feel misunderstood by their parents to find a refuge with a sensitive aunt or uncle, and this might explain why Jesus made first for the Emmatown home. However, the overall impression remains that these two were rather more on the fringe of things. They were followers of Jesus who had 'hoped' rather than been convinced that he was going to be the national liberator. They would perhaps have been found regularly among the crowd whenever Jesus gave his public teaching. But they had not been present at the more private sessions between Jesus and his friends when he had explained to them that he would suffer. These ideas came as new to them and as a revelation. They had followed with dismay the events of Good Friday, but their knowledge of events they shared with all the other visitors to Jerusalem at that time, for whom the fate of Jesus was the main topic of interest and conversation. They were sufficiently informed to know how to find the disciples and close enough to have caught the rumours of the empty tomb. But the walk to Emmatown looks somewhat like the dispersal of the crowd after an accident has been cleared up and the ambulance taken the injured away.

Christians are still slowly and painfully freeing themselves from debilitating prejudices that for centuries have blinded them to truths which otherwise would have been obvious. It will surely become easier as the twenty-first century progresses to consider the possibility that the Emmatown couple were gay. Traditionally the two have always been portrayed by artists as a single sex couple and may be this tradition conveys an unspoken understanding. If so, the story takes on a different meaning and begins to say other things. In the second part of his work, Luke tells the story of a castrated man who also makes a journey away from Jerusalem to his home in a spirit of disappointment and frustration. (Acts 8: 26) Like the Emmaus pair, he is miraculously joined by a stranger who relates the good news to his condition. There are no barriers of sex or sexuality as far as Jesus is concerned, nor for his true followers. In the one story a deviant couple are drawn back to the community of Jesus' friends to add their experience to the life of the whole; in the other story a deviant black man takes his experience of the including love of God back to his own community. We have the sketchy evidence of a first century Gay Christian Movement, which, like its contemporary counterpart, both offers enlightenment to the Church and conveys the Good News of Jesus to those the Church has rejected. Jesus in one case, a freelance evangelist in another, bypass the Church's officialdom in order to bring joy to downcast and downtrodden.

Now we come to the greatest mystery of all – the failure of the two to recognize Jesus as they journeyed together. If the mystery were confined to this particular appearance, then we could just about conjure up enough by way of explanation. The journey took place in failing light; the stranger perhaps wore a cowl; in any case they did not know Jesus that well, had perhaps only seen him before from the edge of the crowd. This was not the age of television and close-ups, and it was before the invention of spectacles. Poor eyesight was and still is common in the Middle East. Likewise there was no electricity. The homestead would have been lit by a flickering oil lamp. No such factors adequately explain why Maggie mistook her nearest and dearest for the gardener; why other close friends in Galilee failed to recognize the stranger on the shore; nor why Twin recognized Jesus not by his face but by his hands and side; nor when the eleven met Jesus on the mountain "some doubted". (Matthew 28:17) Taken together these instances form a pattern. The risen Jesus was not immediately recognizable by his features but only discerned by other means. Something important is being said about the body of Jesus, and to this we shall return in the next study.

There is an on-going historical/scientific debate concerning the nature of the Resurrection – historical reality or apprehension of faith? Physical or spiritual? Natural or supernatural? And so on. In all this we tend to assume that however divided we may be, there was for the first Christians a common reality, a common experience, a common way of understanding the Resurrection. This is unlikely, just as it is unlikely that there was a common understanding of any other item of Christian doctrine.

What we have portrayed in the Emmatown story may be a way of understanding the Resurrection that has not had much of a following in subsequent Christian theology and whose time for revival may still lie somewhere in the future. The notion of re-incarnation we associate with Hinduism and Buddhism. It was also a popular notion in the time of Jesus, though probably not considered to be orthodox Jewish doctrine. Herod was afraid that Jesus was John the Dipper risen from the dead. (Mark 6:16) though his spies could have told him that they did not look alike, to say nothing of clothing or style. Some popular opinion sided with the view of Herod, whereas others believed Jesus was Elijah, Jeremiah or one of the prophets. (Matthew 17:11&12) Jesus believed that John the Dipper was Elijah. John saw himself as the anonymous prophet of Babylon. (John 1:19-23) When the disciples asked Jesus if the man born blind had sinned or his parents, the reply of Jesus refuted the view that a simple connection can be made between individual sin and misfortune, but he did not thereby contradict the view that the man might have had a previous existence. (John 9:1-4) The notion of reincarnation may stand behind Jesus' 'inasmuch' with reference to the treatment of other people.

> **"I remember when I was thirsty, and you brought me a drink; once I was a social outcast, and you invited me home; then I had nothing decent to wear, and you kitted me out; when I was unwell, you looked after me and when I was in prison, you visited me…"** (Matthew 25)

We take these words metaphorically. The needy person is a 'stand in' or substitute for Jesus. In so doing we may be robbing the words of their original force. The first Christians felt the need to be awake, alert, on the look out for the real presence of the living, Resurrected Jesus, incarnate in the stranger who needs help. (See also Mark 9:36 – the little child) It explains the enthusiasm among the first Christians for the practice of hospitality (Romans 12:13 & Hebrews 13:2) and their concern for those in prison (Hebrews 13:3), neither of which receives such prominence among Christians today. In the same way we do not get the full impact of the first Christians' understanding of what it means to be indwelt by the spirit of Jesus because we do not share the popular belief in spirit-possession current at the time. Christians of those days identified Jesus in other people and sought to embody the risen and living Jesus within themselves. Our metaphorical understanding is inadequate to express their experience.

The Emmatown couple had communion with Jesus because they invited a stranger into their home. It is an important point in the story that had they not done so the joy of the Resurrection would have been denied them. They had to put gentle pressure on the stranger to come in. The initiative was with them. So often we do not respond to the call of the needy until they make themselves a nuisance. We oblige them to whinge and complain; we put them in the embarrassing position of having to solicit our help.

The climax of the story is the recognition of the stranger as the risen Jesus at the communion table. The connection between the communion and the recognition of Jesus could not be clearer. The communion formula is complete – he 'took', 'blessed', 'broke' and 'gave'. 'At that moment they realized who he was.' But the communion is closely linked with the preparation for it.

> **"What a wonderful experience that was! How he cheered us up on that walk together! We understood the old books for the first time!"**

The celebration of Holy Communion is preceded by preaching. Preaching and sacrament join together with the sacrament of service to make a complete whole. A Jesus-centred explanation of the scriptures is a good overture to a meal with him, surpassing any time-honoured or recently clobbered together liturgy. Whilst the sacrament of food and drink must never be smothered with words, the gift of language must be recognized as one of God's greatest gifts to the human species. Yet without sensitivity that responds to the needs of the stranger, word and sacrament are dust and ashes.

However they understood it, the Emmatown couple perceived the presence of Jesus in the breaking of bread. It is unlikely they had been at the Last Supper, though they may have been present on one of the other occasions when Jesus had presided at a communion meal. So for these two the broken bread does not principally signify the body of Jesus on the cross, but rather is a sign of his risen presence. Even if they were not acquainted with the physical features of Jesus, they knew of his way of handling and breaking the bread, so that it could be the trigger that produced recognition and joy. Emmatown is Bethel revisited. The gate of heaven is opened and the light of a new age breaks in. As with Jacob, the excitement lingers long after the experience itself.

With the Emmatown couple we must firmly link the celebration of communion with the Easter experience. At the breaking of bread it is the risen Jesus who comes to our consciousness to set our hearts alight with love for him in everyone we encounter along the road.

OC10-12

CHAPTER TEN

IN THE FLESH

'While they were talking, they suddenly realized that Jesus was there with them. Jesus said, "Calm down." They were frightened and thought they were seeing a ghost. Jesus said, "Why are you so nervous? What's the problem? It really is me. Look at my hands and my feet. You can touch me if you like. Ghosts don't have flesh and bones like me." Then he let them have good look at his hands and his feet. They were very happy to see him, but still found it difficult to believe. Jesus said, "I could do with something to eat." They brought him some grilled fish and part of a honeycomb. He took the food and eat it while they watched.' (Luke 2: 36-43)

AT last, at the very end of the first Easter Sunday, Jesus appeared to the official disciple band. Although rumours had been flying around all day, the appearance took the friends by surprise and off their guard. Thus we are gently reminded that there is a big difference between a faith that is pious wishful thinking and one that has the sure conviction that what is commonly regarded as impossible can actually happen. It is no wonder that liberal Christians, myself included, feel uneasy when faced with the Resurrection stories, for they question, more than any other part of the scripture, the nature of our faith and indeed its very reality. If it is of any comfort, the first friends of Jesus seem on this score to have been much closer in temperament to modern liberal and radical Christians, more prone to doubt, than to those who are confident that they are in possession of the complete programme of what God has done, is doing, and is about to do. But we must take seriously the accusations of our blessedly assured critics that our brand of faith is not the real thing and that we are only paddling in the shallows. We are loathe to face up to the fundamental incredibility of the Christian message.

The story of the Resurrection is just as incredible as Gulliver's Travels or the Book of Mormon, though considerably less bizarre than either. It constitutes a challenge, a hurdle, a stumbling block to belief. We seem, our critics suggest, to be wanting to have it both ways. We value and seek to promote the love, joy, peace and hope for the world that flow from the Jesus story, but at the same time our minds wish to suspend belief and our hearts avoid conviction that there is any concrete reality to the events on which that love, joy, peace and hope are stated by scripture to be based. Like the first disciples we are called upon to believe the unbelievable. For it was at the point where the unbelievable was believed that the history of the Christian community, our community, began. Like the first disciples, we find belief difficult, but there is no trick of the mind, no series of academic acrobatics that can rescue us from the challenge. If we dodge we are in no position to accuse other people of intellectual dishonesty. There are many ways in which the Christian faith can and should be made more comprehensible and relevant to the people of our age. But there is no way in which the prime step of faith can be made easy. We are asked to believe that someone who was dead, cold dead, stone dead, is risen and alive for evermore!

It is in the context of this crisis of belief that the second communion of Easter Day was celebrated. The friends displayed no alarm at the reports and rumours from others that Jesus had risen – this they could cope with. The reports produced, possibly, feelings of warmth and consolation. But when Jesus appeared to ***them***, the experience was uncomfortable in the extreme. The first words of Jesus were, "Calm down", and we are flashed back to the Sea of Galilee and the storm and the panic that required similar words from Jesus. (Mark 4:39) The terror of the unknown and the unprepared for gripped them once again, and Jesus had to ask, "Why are you so nervous?" The risen presence of Jesus played havoc with the minds and emotions of the friends. How could it be otherwise when beings endowed with reason are confronted by the incredible? This is not kid's stuff. Anyone today having such an experience would perhaps wish to offer themselves as a voluntary patient in a psychiatric unit. When faced with a situation totally alien to any previous experience, the human mind will either crack or it will struggle to find some explanation, some category into which the experience can be put that will enable it to cope. Visions, fantasies, even the possibility of an extra-terrestrial visitation are more acceptable than the real thing. However, the doubts that Jesus sought to allay on this occasion seem not so much to do with intellectual objections as with emotional inadequacy. In the equivalent account in John's gospel, the crisis of belief centres on Twin who the writer portrays as the archetypal doubter in much the same way as Judas is understood as the archetypal traitor. For Twin the crisis is an intellectual one- he demands scientific proof. (John 20:5) But Luke sees the doubts as psychological as well, and thus even more difficult to overcome. When Twin saw the evidence he had asked for – Jesus' wounds – he believed. Not so the disciples in Luke. Jesus showed them his hands and his feet and they still could not believe. And what they doubt at this point is their emotional state, which has changed from fear to happiness, but is none the less off balance and not to be trusted. The friends mistrust ecstasy just as Twin, with equal wisdom, mistrusts irrationality as a foundation for belief. Belief must be based on reality, however incredible that reality may be.

An impasse had been reached. The response of Jesus was to celebrate Communion. He said, "I could do with something to eat!" Immediately we are on familiar ground. There are similar requests from Jesus to the disciples to provide food preceding the feeding of the five thousand and the four thousand. We are also reminded of Jesus' request to the Samaritan woman, "Give me a drink." It is the familiar gesture of calling for whatever food or drink is at hand, however sparse or inadequate, and using it for communion. Jesus is offered boiled fish, presumably the left-overs from suppertime. (Fish is still the customary meal for Jews at the end of the Sabbath, in the form of a kind of fishcake.) This Jesus 'took and ate'. Again we note the communion language. Jesus shared the disciples' food: the bond of friendship is re-established. But this aspect of the event is secondary to the more pressing need to convince the disciples of his resurrection. The procedure Jesus adopts is aimed squarely at eliminating alternative explanations to the phenomenon of his appearance with which the friends are struggling to hold on to reality as they have up to this point understood it. They could be seeing a ghost, a spirit. As Jews they believed in Hades where the departed had a shadowy minimal degree of existence whence they could, under special circumstances make a brief re-appearance, as did Samuel. (1 Samuel 28:3) Such appearances were against the natural order of things, disturbing and spooky, and they usually warned of some imminent disaster. In no way could an appearance of Jesus as a ghost be regarded as a resurrection. Hades was not the abode of the living but the dead. By resurrection the Jews of the time understood a complete restoration of the physical being of the deceased with all attendant faculties and properties. Nothing less would do.

Today, since our understanding of the universe is different from that of the first century, there are many who feel more comfortable with some kind of 'spiritual' resurrection, rather than the form of resurrection Luke is very anxious to assert in his account. The words 'spiritual' and 'physical' are difficult because straightway we are into the game of 'it all depends what you mean' by physical /spiritual. The first disciples' idea of the spiritual in relation to Jesus was very different from the ideas of a twentieth century theologian arguing for a spiritual resurrection. The way a contemporary spiritualist understands things is quite different again. Nonetheless, those who use the word 'spiritual' in contradiction to the word 'physical', however they understand the expressions, are in danger of making the Resurrection of Jesus less real and less part of the real world than Luke and the other gospel writers intend us to understand it. The line taken by Bultmann and many others who have followed him, that whether the Resurrection stories have any value as history is irrelevant, and that it is only the theological truths enshrined therein and the faith of the believer that count, does not constitute a denial of the Resurrection as some suppose, nor indeed of miracles. But this particular way of seeking to make the faith more accessible to doubters does have serious implications for the place of Christianity as a historical religion, firmly rooted and grounded in this world, with a real incarnation of flesh and blood and a real resurrection of flesh and blood also. The witness of the Christian scriptures is that God chooses to work in **this** world, in terms of the life and experience and reality of which we are a part, and not in some parallel spiritual world apprehended by the mind, however sophisticated or devout. Spiritualizing the Resurrection does not constitute a sound platform for Christians who seek social and political reform, but rather for those who wish to keep their New Jerusalem firmly out of this world. It is no accident that Bultmann was soft on Fascism.

According to Luke, the Resurrection body of Jesus was accessible to the human senses. Jesus could be seen, heard and touched. "Ghosts don't have flesh and bones like me." But in case there should be any doubts, (might not Jesus be tangible on the outside, but hollow on the inside?) Jesus goes on to demonstrate that he has a digestive system. This is incredible, but Luke challenges us to accept it as the truth. So our celebrations of Holy Communion bear witness to a Jesus who exists as part of the same reality of which we are part, who feels and tastes in the same way as we do. How else could true communion take place? This does not exhaust the gospel-writer's understanding of Jesus' Resurrection body. Whilst there is a common denominator of flesh and blood and of the senses, making communion possible, there are also factors that speak of transformation. The theme of delayed recognition does not feature as prominently in this story as in the others, though it is implied in the assuring "It really is me". However Jesus did not come in through the door. The friends simply realized that Jesus was there while they were talking. He had earlier disappeared from the sight of the Emmatown couple, now to re-appear almost simultaneously on their arrival back in Jerusalem. This time they had not seen him on the way. The conquest of death is accompanied by the conquest of the limitations of time and space. These hints of a heightened form of existence are restrained and delicate so as to avoid foolish rhapsodising on the nature of the after life. It is in much the same vein that Paul in his first letter to the Christians in Corinth meets speculation as to the form of the Resurrection body.

> **'I can hear someone asking, "How can the dead come back to life? What sort of body do they have?" That's a silly question, but I'll try to answer it.'** (Ist Letter to Corinth, chapter 15 verse 35 Good As New.)

Paul makes clear that he understands the resurrection life of Jesus, which is that intended for the whole human race, to involve a body, thus preserving the link with our present experience of the way we communicate and relate to one another. But it is a transformed body, one that takes us beyond the limits of what at present understand and experience. "We shall all undergo a change," he tells us. It is important to grasp that for Paul physical and spiritual are not opposites. The spiritual includes the physical and is an extension of it into a new dimension. "The bodies we have now which die and rot, will have a new form, so they'll never die or rot."

The Good News Meal is, above all, a celebration of the Resurrection of Jesus. By its means the incredible is affirmed within the realm of our reality, not in order to indicate an alternative reality, but to transform radically our view of the reality of here and now. The Resurrection of Jesus is not consolatory but revolutionary. It is not a phenomenon private to Jesus himself. Jesus is the prototype of what is now to be acknowledged as the future for everybody.

Holy Communion is also a celebration of the physical. We use physical things such as bread and wine, and witness to Jesus, someone who has flesh and blood. The sacramental depends on the physical. From the very beginning Christianity had to contend with the heresy of Gnosticism in its many forms, which ascribed to the physical a lower status than the spiritual, even in some forms an evil anti-God status. There is no expression of Christianity today entirely unaffected by this heresy. It accounts for the guilt Christians feel when they enjoy life, especially those pleasures thought of as 'sensual'. It accounts for half-heartedness in the championship of causes that have to do with conservation of the natural world and the earth's resources, as well as the promotion and appreciation of art and culture – these things are done with greater enthusiasm by pagans. We also adopt a superior attitude to those who are over-meticulous or sentimental in arrangements for burying the dead. We are programmed to feel that all these things have to do with a world that is passing away, and detract from our quest for the life to come, which has nothing to do with bodies or bones or anything so material.

On Easter Day, Jesus stood in a body of flesh and blood to re-affirm the verdict of God that everything God has made is good. Jesus ate fish that was good to taste and good for the digestive system. Some manuscripts also include a honeycomb in the meal, an important touch retained in the

King James' Version, J.B. Phillips and Good As New. It is the sweet to compliment the savoury. Eating is not only a necessity but also a pleasure. (Some believe that those in the early Christian communities who were dipped at Eastertime were given a mixture of milk and honey to symbolize their crossing of the Jordan into Canaan. A new Exodus had taken place; the food of bitterness left behind.) What God has made God holds to be of eternal value. Those things we understand as physical have a place in God's future, a future that will also include things not yet within our realm of experience. (1 Corinthians 2:9)

As with the first disciples, belief in the Resurrection of Jesus, and in the eternal future for all humankind of which it is the guarantee, remains stubbornly difficult for us no matter how much we may preach or debate it. No matter how great our Christian commitment, the meeting with Jesus face to face will come as a surprise as it did for Maggie and Clover and Twin. We will best prepare ourselves for that eventuality not by flights of fancy into the spiritual realm, but by being joyful participants in the here and now, by eating and drinking the bread and the fish, the honey and the wine.

I DON'T KNOW WHY

I don't know why God's mighty love
To this world was made known;
Nor why to hard, ungrateful hearts
Such kindness has been shown.

But I've read the Jesus story-
Hope for the losers, cheer for the lonely;
I know that love's forever-
It will last beyond all time.

I don't know how God's Spirit moves
Directing love and life;
Nor why the world's so beautiful
Despite its pain and strife.

But I've felt her gentle thrilling
In music's rhythms and poet's meaning;
When any high endeavour
Transforms the gloom and grime.

I don't know what the future holds
Or how the end will come;
If God has more for me to do,
Or if my work is done.

But it's good to have a part in
God's work- creating, befriending, sharing.
I've seen the Bright World's colour,
And it's going to be fine!

(After 'I know not why God's wondrous grace' D.W. Whittle, 1840-1901)

CHAPTER ELEVEN

GRAND FINALE

'Some time later Jesus met his friends again by the lake in Galilee. This is how it happened. Rocky, Twin, Nathan from nearby Cana, Zebedee's boys (James and John), and two other friends met together. Rocky said, "I'm going fishing." The others said, "A good idea!" So they took the boat out onto the lake. But although they worked hard all night, they didn't catch anything.

Early in the morning Jesus came down to the beach, but the friends did not recognize him. Jesus called out, "Have you caught any fish, boys?" They called back, "Not a thing!" Jesus shouted, "You'll catch something if you cast your nets over there to the right!" They threw the net where Jesus was pointing and they could not pull it back in again - it was so full of fish. The friend Jesus had a special love for said to Rocky, "Its the Leader!" Rocky had no clothes on, so when he realized Jesus was there he grabbed his cloak and dived into the water. The other friends came on in the boat, pulling the net full of fish behind them. They were not far from the beach, within easy shouting distance.

When they came on to the beach, they saw a barbecue fire with some fish being cooked, and some bread beside it. Jesus said, "We could do with some of the fish you've just caught as well." So Rocky went back into the boat and dragged the net onto the beach. It was full of large fish, a hundred and fifty three. Although there were so many, the net was not torn. Jesus said, "Time for breakfast!" None of the friends needed to ask Jesus, "What's your name?" They knew it was their leader. Jesus came close to them, took the bread and gave it to them. Then he handed round the fish. This makes the third time Jesus had met with his friends after he had come back to life.

After breakfast Jesus had a talk with Rocky. "Simon Johnson, do you have a strong love for me - more than these other friends of mine?" Rocky said, "You must know, Leader, how strong my feelings are for you!" Jesus said, "Look after the weak people I care about." Jesus asked Rocky again, "Simon Johnson, do you love me? " Rocky said, "Of course, Leader, you know I'm your friend!" Jesus said, "I want you to look after my tough people too!" The third time Jesus said, "So you're my friend, are you?" Rocky was hurt because Jesus asked him three times about his feelings for him. Rocky said, "Leader, you know everything about me. You know I love you as a friend!" Jesus said to him, "You've got to have enough love to meet the needs of all my people! The problem is that up to now you've lived just like a teenage delinquent, doing up your belt and going off wherever you fancied. When you're old, you'll have to stretch out your hands and someone else will tie a belt around you and force you to go where you don't want to." (Jesus was giving Rocky a clue as to how he would die in the cause of God.) Then Jesus said, "You'd better stay close to me!"

Rocky looked round and saw the friend Jesus had a special love for, just behind them. (This was the friend who snuggled up close to Jesus when they were having a meal and asked Jesus who the traitor was.) When Rocky saw him, he said to Jesus, "What about him, Leader?" Jesus said. "I may want him to hang around till I come for him, but that's none of your business. You stay close to me!" (John 21. Good News from Sources Close to Jesus.)

THE last chapter of Sources Close (traditionally known as John) appears to be a kind of appendix, possibly supplied by another hand, albeit of the same theological school of thought as the writer of the other chapters. It complements the Resurrection appearances of Jesus in Jerusalem, recorded in chapter 20, with an appearance in Galilee. This is in line with the words towards the end of Mark's Good News as we now have it, spoken by the well-dressed young man, possibly Mark himself, "Go and tell his friends, including Rocky, he plans to go ahead of you to Galilee, just as he said he would. You'll meet him there." (Mark 16:7 compare Mark 14:28) It looks as if the end of Mark's work is irretrievably lost, but it may have contained an account of the incident recorded in Sources 21. Indeed, Sources 21 could be the lost ending of Mark re-worked to give it its own particular emphasis. It is possible also that Luke had access to the lost ending, for he records an account of a great catch of fish under the direction of Jesus earlier in his version of the Good News at the point when Rocky received his first call (Luke 5: 6 & 7) Luke omits any reference to Galilean Resurrection appearances in his books, giving the impression that the Galilean friends of Jesus remained in Jerusalem from Easter to Pentecost. So in his scheme of things there is no room for an Eastertide miracle in Galilee. Yet it is too good a story to omit. The fact that Mark's Good News, by tradition using Rocky's reminiscences, does not mention such a miracle to accompany Rocky's first call, arouses the suspicion that Luke does not have right context for the story. Although there are minor differences in detail, the overall pattern of the stories in Luke 5 and Sources 21 is similar. The disciples have worked hard all night and have not caught anything. By obeying the instructions of Jesus they land a bumper catch, causing problems of handling in each case. Both conclude with an intimate scene between Jesus and Rocky in which Rocky's guilt is aroused and then set aside by a vote of confidence from Jesus who calls him personally to be an evangelist and pastor. Rocky's guilt makes more sense as a consequence of his denial. The writer of Sources 21 skilfully harks back to that moment of shame in his report of Jesus' threefold questioning of Rocky as to the sincerity of his love. (Rocky's anxiety to cover his genitals reminds us of Adam and Eve whose similar behaviour symbolizes guilt. Some interpret Rocky's drawing his coat about him as preparation to meet Jesus and his jumping into the sea as impatience to get to land. It seems more likely to have been an instinctive and clumsy attempt to hide from Jesus what he had proudly been flaunting to his companions.) Rocky's confession of guilt in the context in which Luke places it, is somewhat out of character, for before the events of Good Friday and Easter Rocky is usually portrayed as being macho, self-assured, and lacking in humility. In both accounts miracle and parable merge, the successful landing of fish being a symbol of the disciples' mission.

In all this, problems of leadership and organization in the early Church seem to be reflected. There is the problem of Rocky's authority. It may be that some were reluctant to accept his leadership in view of his behaviour in the Palace courtyard. Others, perhaps, whilst accepting that Jesus had forgiven and re-instated him to the inner circle of friends, believed he was still too big for his boots. In Luke, Rocky cannot land the catch on his own, but needs to call on the help of the sons of Zebedee, and even then both boats are in danger of sinking! Is this a plea for greater democracy, a more wide-spreading of the load of responsibility among the first Christians? Similarly, in Sources, Rocky needs the other disciples. His impetuous, headstrong assertion, "I'm going fishing" is followed by the others making sure they are in on the act, "A good idea!" Throughout the account, Rocky is upstaged by the figure of 'the friend Jesus had a special love for'. According to the witness of the gospel itself this friend is Larry (Lazarus see Sources 11), who is swifter to spot Jesus than Rocky and who walks close behind Jesus without requiring special attention or encouragement. His place in the subsequent history of the Christian community will be less dramatic but longer lasting than Rocky's own. We see here perhaps the Christians of the Jerusalem suburbs centred on Dategrove (Bethany) asserting their right to be considered as much leaders in the cause of Jesus as the fish magnates from Galilee, especially if it is Larry telling the story.

The change of scene to Galilee, which Luke avoids and which in Sources 21 is a postscript, may perhaps illuminate the politics of the early Church from a different angle. When Luke in his second volume (Acts) records the progress of evangelism following on from the outpouring of the Spirit on the first Whitsunday, the stages are Jerusalem and its vicinity, Samaria and thence to Syro-Phoenicia and Syria, to Asia Minor (modern Turkey), Macedonia, Greece and beyond. This follows the instructions of Jesus at his parting with his friends from Olive Hill. "Your job, when the Spirit gives you confidence, will be to stand up for me in Jerusalem and the surrounding district, in Samaria and all over the world." (Luke's Good News Part Two, chapter 1.) There is no mention of Galilee. The Christian mission leapfrogs over Galilee from Samaria to Damascus, Caesarea and Antioch. There is an obvious reason. Galilee had no need of first-strike evangelism. The area had been thoroughly covered by Jesus himself with his team during his ministry. Galilee was the main scene of Jesus' acts of compassion and healing. The recipients of his message and his personal help were thick on the ground in Galilee. His name was established deep in the hearts and minds of the local inhabitants, even as up in Jerusalem many of the Pentecost pilgrims were hearing that name for the first time. Nor did the Galilean Jesus people keep quiet about their hero and friend. (See Mark 11: 43-45) The presence in the gospels of so many stories of healing and befriending by Jesus bears witness to personal testimonies oft repeated. However, it is not difficult to imagine that Galilean folk Christianity would have had a different emphasis and ethos from that of Jerusalem. The Galileans were Jewish converts from paganism and as such were enthusiastic but somewhat lacking in orthodoxy. The strict set (the Pharisees) obviously had great difficulty in getting them into line, and when Jesus appeared with his message of love and forgiveness they lost any hold they had on the masses entirely. (Mark 1:22) The strict set saw Jesus not as a successful rival in winning the people for God, but as an enemy who had undermined their best efforts to turn the Galileans into a God-fearing, law-abiding people. According to the history of the early Christian communities as recounted by Luke, Jerusalem quickly became the recognized centre of the movement with a community organized and disciplined by twelve apostles, assisted by deacons. Since the Christian message was seen in the first instance as the fulfilment of Jewish hopes, it seemed logical for Jerusalem to become its home. The rapid acceleration in the number of adherents led to problems in providing adequate arrangements for instruction and pastoral care. The apostles had to establish their authority swiftly and keep and eye open for those who might take advantage of any easygoingness for their own ends. Momentous decisions requiring general acceptance had to be taken if there were not to be fatal divisions. These included the procedures for dipping and the recognition of the reception of the Spirit, and the terms for the admission of those Christians who were not starting off as Jews.

One wonders how the Galilean Christians viewed these centralizing tendencies. Did they remind them of the attempts of the strict set to supervise their souls? Taught by Jesus to look for God's New World, to let go their anxieties for the future, to go their ways in peace, trusting the goodness and love of their Parent in heaven, would they sense something not-quite-right about the imposition of rules and regulations by the Jerusalem Church? We cannot know. History is written by the winners. We lack an account of the first years of the Christian communities of Nahum town, Fishtown and Dancetown. We also lack any account of the groups in Dategrove, Figland, Emmatown and Jericho down in the south, which probably had their own, different reasons for being apprehensive about the centralizing tendencies in the capital. Better educated and of a higher social status than their Galilean counterparts, they also had known Jesus intimately and had their stories to tell. Intriguingly the location of Galilee, and a storyteller from the south, combines in Sources 21 to reflect a shared unease, in at least two alternative groups who knew Jesus well, about the way things were going and the behaviour of the official leaders.

According to Matthew, the eleven apostles received their final instructions from Jesus, not in Jerusalem, but on a mountain in Galilee. (Good News from a Jewish Friend

28:16) The Galileans were called back by Jesus to first base! This accords with the witness who reported the events in Sources 21, except that he tells us much more. The grand finale to the ministry of Jesus is the celebration of a communion in the light of the dawn on the lakeside. The authority of Galilee not only survives, but challenges Jerusalem for precedence. It is the authority of personal encounter with and first hand knowledge of Jesus, over against the knowledge conveyed by Church and theological discipline. As such, it is not good against bad, but represents an important strand of Christian understanding that two thousand years of heavy-going ecclesiastical history has not succeeded in breaking. Those who are unhappy with the impression of Jesus they gain through the mediation of the institution need only leave Acts and Paul alone for a while and turn to the pages of the gospels, to the memories of Jesus supplied by his Galilean friends, and get him back into focus.

So the first thing to remark about the Easter Communion in Sources 21 is that it is off centre from the point of view of subsequent ecclesiastical history. 'Galilee of the Gentiles', as it was sometimes called, was close to the border with paganism, and that border was indistinct. (One of their synagogues had been built by a Gentile!) Its people were more interested in Jesus than in theology. (Always a dangerous tendency from the point of view of the institutional Church.) If anything coming out of Jerusalem conflicted with their personal experience of him, they could hardly be expected to be impressed. We are reminded of the communion with the Four Thousand. Jesus spreads his table at the edge to warn against the development of a fixed centre of gravity.

Secondly, the Galilean communion is firmly set in a missionary context. Jesus used the experience of those in the fishing business as a parable of God's New World (Matthew 13:47) and called them to translate that experience into missionary expertise. (Mark 1:17 & 18) Again we must not be sidetracked into the question of the historical accuracy of the miracle, although it is easier to explain on rational grounds than some of the other miracles. Someone standing on the shore might have seen the patterns made by the shoals of fish more easily than those in the boat and could shout out the necessary directions. But it is of the Good News mission that the story speaks, the main point being that we only succeed when we are under the guidance of Jesus himself (not the apostles, especially not Rocky!), for only Jesus is in a position to anticipate where the harvest is likely to be reaped. The specific advice of Jesus to throw the net on the right side of the boat suggests they were casting it on the left. In other words, a radical change in direction was essential for success. This, against the backdrop of a hard night's work of getting nowhere, anticipates the frequent periods in the Church's history when an unresponsive world is blamed for failure in mission, whereas the blame more fittingly lies at the door of a church that is handicapped by lack of imagination and unwillingness to change direction. (The first readers of Sources would probably have taken the advice to mean, "Have a go at the other lot", that is, the Gentiles.) The number 153 is symbolic. It is a good catch but hardly enough to produce the element of miracle and surprise the story suggests, or to cause problems for skilled workers. It is a triangular number and like the number of the Beast in Revelation stands for imperfection. (not perfection as in some commentaries. Square numbers stand for perfection, for example the 144 thousand or the walls and gates of the New Jerusalem.) The 153 must be taken with the comment, 'although there were so many, the net was not torn.' The mission is incomplete. There is plenty of room for more – a warning against the Church's tendency to go for a doctrine of election and practices of exclusivism when it is satisfied with the number and type of its clientele. The instructions of Jesus in Matthew 28, also in the Galilean setting, are thus preserved in parable form in Sources 21. But the themes are the same- the authority of Jesus, the assurance of his presence, and the universality of the mission.

It is worth noting the missionary context for the Galilean communion. There has often been a polarization between those churches and communities that emphasise sacramental worship and those who practice evangelism. Mission is the proper context for eating and drinking with Jesus, and such celebration is the reward and climax of mission undertaken in his spirit. Fish are brought to land, and fish are used by Jesus in the communion meal. Fish at the communion not only reminds us of the Resurrection presence of Jesus, but is also the symbol of those newly won, fresh, gleaming friends of Jesus, fished from right outside the Christian community. If a church never has any of these to offer, it should ask itself whether it is time to try the other side of the boat, or even, like Rocky, to jump out of the boat altogether! The hard work and enthusiasm of evangelicals is a fit cause for admiration and inspiration. The problem for them (and I claim my place among them) is that, beginning with the assumption that they have got the message right, the only answer to failure or limited success is to work harder, shout louder and be more aggressive. Whereas a simple admission, that in this or that respect they may have failed to interpret correctly the mind of Jesus, might work wonders and render unnecessary so called 'aggressive evangelism' (a contradiction in terms if ever there was one.)

And now to the communion itself. There is a magic atmosphere. The disciples are tired but fulfilled. They meet with Jesus, unexpectedly, in the early morning light and the fresh morning breezes. Jesus is the host, as in every true communion. He issues the invitation, "Time for breakfast!" and although there are plenty of fish in the boat, Jesus has himself provided the meal because the fish is already cooking when they arrive on shore. Jesus as host provides, invites and presides. This is a warning to priests and churches that look upon the altar as **their** table. It is Jesus' Table. Churches still continue to turn people away from their table. Those who come to Jesus are never turned away (Sources 6:37) Bread and fish are the food, but fish seems to be given greater prominence. 'They saw a barbecue fire with some fish being cooked, and some bread beside it.' Thus the sign of the Resurrection is to the fore. The communion language is clear. Jesus 'takes' the bread, 'gives it' to them, and the fish 'in the same way'. A first century barbecue! But without the artificial out-of-doors/back-to-nature of today's barbecuing middle classes! These folk were enjoying a simple meal in what was for them the most natural of surroundings. There was no tablecloth, no candles or music, no incense other than the sweet smell of cooking. Communion with Jesus is a simple meal and cannot be improved upon by elaboration.

It is time to bring the element of fish back into the communion. It is especially appropriate for the season of Easter to Pentecost. Short of organizing a barbecue at the seaside, which some climates do not encourage at that time of the year, there are many ways in which the fish can be introduced. Some churches already combine an Easter breakfast with a celebration of communion at the breakfast table, with fish fingers, kippers or sardines, not forgetting honey in a comb, served as part of the meal. Not everyone likes fish and the position of vegetarians and vegans must be respected, as also total abstainers with regard to the wine. Communion requires sensitivity in these matters. Availability on the menu is the key; ***not*** making it an essential element for all. When as a group of friends we eat together in a restaurant, we do not all eat the same food, yet we share the meal. Bread or biscuits in the shape of fish is a possible alternative. I have often used white chocolate in the shape of little fishes, especially popular with the children, but not spurned by the adults either! If the offering of fish is part of a more conventional celebration of communion, then embarrassment can be avoided if pieces of bread and fish are served on either side of the same plate and people may take both or just the bread as they wish. The traditional wafers used in Catholic and Anglican churches could be made into the shape of a fish for the Easter period. The widening of the menu to include fish depends on an acceptance of all the communions of Jesus in the gospels as authoritative for understanding and practice. When the fish re-appears on the table in some form or another we will know the penny has dropped!

The most astounding feature of the communion in Galilee – a constant feature in all the communions of Jesus, but here highlighted by the events of the Passion and Easter – is the character of the communicants and their spiritual state. The guests on the beach were failures every one. They had recently forsaken their leader, and abandoned his ideals at the critical moment. That they could not make a decent catch of fish until Jesus turned up seems to symbolize their failure. Indeed, some commentators have seen the decision to embark on the fishing expedition, rather than wait for the promised arrival of Jesus and his instructions, as an act of self-will. Rocky is the number one culprit here, as also it is he who suffers the worst pangs of guilt by dint of his denial. He cannot do anything right. The theme of Rocky's guilt runs through the story,- a guilt that is self-inflicted and self-perpetuated, of course. After the comical leap into the sea, Rocky is the one who goes back to the boat to busy himself with the nets and the catch, putting off the moment when he must come face to face with Jesus. Yet Jesus is not interested in giving Rocky a session of pastoral counselling until the meal is over. First things first! The Good News order is that guilty sinners are invited to the banquet of God's New

World, receiving thereby the assurance of God's love and acceptance, **before** the business of confession and repentance. The idea that we must be shriven and clean behind the ears before we are fit to have communion with God is anti-Gospel; and also impractical. We shall not be clean when we take the food and drink, even if we confess up to the last moment before swallowing. The Good News is that it doesn't matter. Jesus accepts us as we are, and then begins his work of grace. We have to get this straight because not only does it affect our own relationship with Jesus, which includes his direction to drop our anxiety, but has an important bearing on our relationship with other people. Our reluctance to accept and embrace other sinners in their sins is tied up with our own faulty assumption of cleanliness as we approach God, the essence of Pharisaism. The fact that we have been through some form of vetting process, whether in liturgical form or in the form of a priestly analyst's couch, does not make us more fit to be in Jesus' company than anyone else, and we are committing another sin if we think so. Such procedures put our minds at rest, but it is doubtful if they should. What should put our minds at rest is the Good News – "He spends his time with disreputable types of people and even has meals with them!" (Luke 15:2)

There is an old story from Scotland of a woman of dubious reputation who chanced to enter a kirk at the time of a communion service. When the bread was brought round to her she sadly shook her head. The elder, recognizing here, pushed the plate in front of her, "Och, take it lassie, it's for sinners."

JESUS, IT SURELY CAN'T BE TRUE

Jesus, it surely can't be true
That someone is ashamed of you?
Ashamed of one all great hearts praise?
Whose story sounds through endless days?
Ashamed of Jesus?- sooner far
Let evening blush to own a star;
You send bright beams of light divine
To chase away those clouds of mine!

Ashamed of Jesus, dearest friend,
On whom my peace and joy depend?
No! When I blush, this is my shame-
That I so rarely speak his name!

Ashamed of Jesus? Yes I may-
When I've no faults to hide away,
No one to comfort or relieve,
No truth to learn, no good to achieve.

To save the world, you died in pain;
With life for all, you rose again;
This is the truth that sets us free-
Jesus is not ashamed of me!

(After Joseph Grigg 1722-68 and Benjamin Francis 1734-99.
Tunes Ombersley or Eisenach)

CHAPTER TWELVE

HIS FIRST COMMUNION

'In the beginning God spoke. This is just like God - part of the way God is. Everything there is comes from God speaking; otherwise there would be nothing at all. God speaking brought into being the life and intelligence we all share. These have kept on shining like light in the darkness and have never been defeated by the darkness. There was a messenger from God called John. John played his part in keeping the light shining, encouraging people to trust the light, although he was not the light himself. The full light that makes things clear to everybody was then coming into the world. The one who made the world appeared in the world, but the world paid no attention. Those specially prepared, God's chosen people, turned

their backs. Nevertheless there were many who opened their arms in trust, and these are the rightful children of God. They are not children in the human sense, the result of family planning or physical passion, but in the sense of sharing God's nature. God spoke by means of a human being living among us. We have seen the beauty of the only complete physical expression of The Loving God, wonderful to look at and to know. John showed his support by shouting out, "This is the one I was telling you about, 'The one who arrives after me is more important than me, because he existed before me.' " From his superstore we have received one good gift after another. Moses gave us rules and regulations: Jesus, God's representative, gave us true love. No one has ever seen God, but the one faithful likeness who shares God's nature has shown us what God is like.' (John Chapter One. Good As New)

'One day Jesus saw some mothers feeding their babies at the breast. Jesus said to his friends, "Little babies are the perfect example for those who want to be citizens of God's New World." The friends said, "Surely we don't have to become babies in order to qualify for the New World?" Jesus replied, "When two people become one, like a mother feeding her child; when there's no difference between the way you behave and what's going on in your mind, or between your head and your heart; when you treat males and females equally, without any distinctions whatsoever; when you respond naturally to another's body language; when you accept people as they are – then you'll be ready for God's New World." ' (Thomas v.22)

'You must be like babies who've just been born. Like babies who feed naturally from their mother's breast, you must think of God as your mother and seek God's nourishment. Then you'll grow to a full and complete life. Have you tasted how good God is?' (Good As New 'The Call to Hope' 1 Peter Chapter 2)

IT'S odd when you come to think of it that we allow our imaginations to work hard thinking about that stable in Bethlehem. What sort of accommodation did Mary and Joseph have? Was it smelly? Was the straw clean? But we don't often wonder what they had to eat. Did the provisions of the hotel spill over to include the outhouse? Was it possible to order a 'take-away'? "If I were a shepherd, I would bring a lamb". Pretty picture, isn't it, the cuddly lamb in the shepherd's arms on the Christmas cards. But if the shepherd brought a lamb it would not have been for a pet. Joseph or the Innkeeper would have killed it according to Jewish custom, draining off the blood, and then it would have provided food for several days perhaps, roast or boiled, seasoned with herbs and spices. Various dried fruits- figs, raisins, dates, would have served as accompaniments. John the Baptist called Jesus 'God's Lamb'. It's a title that has stuck. Not only is it a picture of the way Jesus gave his life for others, it also identifies Jesus with the death and the suffering still undergone by animals in order to keep us alive or satisfy our appetites.

A few years ago, Valerie and I had a few days holiday in Skegness. One day we visited a children's zoo. It was very well set out and very animal friendly, as I remember. Many of the animals were freely wandering throughout the enclosed area. We stopped by one little paddock with a very low wall and could see nothing inside. Then I heard a voice very close to my left elbow say, "ELLOW". I turned to find I was being addressed by a very friendly turkey who had either been schooled to say 'hello' by the keeper, or had picked it up from the constant stream of visitors. He also tried very hard to engage us in conversation with his gobble-gobble language that sounded very much an imitation of human speech. He would nuzzle up to you and was quite happy to be stroked. It is not easy to eat an animal who has greeted you with a friendly 'hello'. Perhaps one day we shall come to identify Jesus not only with the sufferings of humanity, as we should, but with the suffering of all those turkeys factory-bred for our pleasure at Christmas. The Word became flesh - not just human flesh, but the flesh all living creatures have in common.

But as to Jesus himself, and what food he had at the first Christmas, we don't have to speculate. He had his mother's milk. It is proving a struggle to relearn these days what should be obvious, that breast-feeding is the most natural, most healthy and most hygienic way of feeding a baby. It is now always recommended unless there are exceptional problems, although as I have discovered in the case of my grandchildren born in hospital, the staff are so stretched that frequently they are unable to give the time and the support necessary to mothers seeking to breast feed. Our local chapel here in Taffs Well has just provided a room for breast feeding mothers to meet one another and feed their little ones. A great idea!

I hope, dear reader, you are keeping up your boycott of Nestlé products as urged by the World Health Organisation and the World Council of churches. Babies are still dying because Nestlés are marketing powdered milk in areas where mothers don't have the facilities or the right education for proper sterilization. We throw up our hands over the 'commercialization of Christmas' and bemoan our inability to do anything about it. Nestlés profits have been significantly dented by the boycott. But if Christians everywhere were to stand firm, shoulder to shoulder, there is no doubt that Nestlés would have to change its policy or go under. We have the power to change things if we want to. The only problem is the weakness of our moral sensitivities.

I like to sing the full version of Christina Rossetti's poem 'In the bleak mid-winter'. Baptists (my own tribe!) are not encouraged to sing the whole carol. In our hymnbook, and in other hymnbooks too, the words 'a breastful of milk' have encountered the censor's knife. It's tragic that so many Christians have been brought up in such a way that they cannot contemplate the naked human body except in terms of embarrassment or as an object of temptation and lust. We are sick! Out has also gone the second verse of Wesley's great hymn 'Love divine, all loves excelling'. I play the organ for services sometimes. Instinctively after the mezzo-forte of the first verse I push in some stops in readiness for a quieter, more reflective, verse. Instead of which the congregation has braced itself for 'Come almighty to deliver..' The symphony has been robbed of its beautiful second movement. ***'Breathe, O breathe your loving spirit into every troubled breast.'*** "No breasts please, we're Baptists!"

There is no more beautiful sight in all the world than a mother breast-feeding her baby. When we sing the full version of 'In the bleak mid-winter', we sing about the first communion of Jesus. Communion means 'sharing'. Jesus began his life of sharing food and drink by sharing that common, life-giving food, which flowed from his mother's breasts into every part of his body. Jesus wasn't squeamish about breasts. According to the Gospel of Thomas (Good As New 'Thought Provoking Sayings of Jesus'), the sight of mothers feeding their babies, inspired Jesus to some telling words about God's New World (The Kingdom).

In a letter he wrote to new Christians, Rocky (Peter), a friend of Jesus, urged his readers to 'crave pure spiritual milk', that is God's milk. There is a startling picture behind these words. New Christians are thought of as babies. And who is their mother from whom they receive this pure milk? Rocky, like Jesus, was a Hebrew, and so thought of God's Spirit as 'she'. (In Hebrew the word spirit is feminine. God is mother as well as father.) At the beginning the newborn baby has to be guided gently to the mother's breast. But after a few times baby gets the idea and then there is no stopping him or her.

Valerie and I had a week in Rome and did all the sights. One of the many things we learnt was that Rocky had a daughter, named Petronilla (Rockette), and that she is buried somewhere in the catacombs. In the early days of the Church, St. Petronilla had a strong cult following which was later discouraged, probably because the idea of Rocky having a wife and family didn't fit well with the Church's teaching on clerical celibacy. (We know Rocky was married, of course, from the gospels and from Paul). I had my hunch confirmed. Rocky's picture of God as a mother feeding her babies is based on his own experience as a father. He says to some new Christians who have just had their bath (baptism) "You new-born babies have had a taste of how good God is. Now have some more; get on with it; get a craving for it; get into the regular habit of feeding at God's breast!"

Think about it. Jesus, God in human flesh, receives human milk from his human mother. Human beings, reborn by God's Spirit, are suckled by God herself! That is the two-way communion we celebrate at Christmas.
God accepts our human food.
We take God's food.
God has joined our family; God has eaten at our table; God is one of us, for always.
We eat at God's table. We share God's food. We have joined God's family.

This means that God is interested in all our concerns, the most critical such as peace on earth down to the most trivial such as the jokes in the Christmas crackers. We also are to be interested in God's concerns, which have always to do with love, joy and peace and their denial in so many parts of his world.

To take the bread and wine, to drink the spiritual milk, is to add an extra dimension to your personality. You are infused with God. You must now see the world not as your selfish playground, not as the stage on which you act out your ambitions and desires, but as the place where you can demonstrate God's love and care, where you can practice and foster the ways of tolerance and understanding, where you can spread happiness and comfort. Just a taste of God, and there's a new world born inside you and all around you. Eat and drink and make merry with God. God will be eating and drinking and making merry with you.

CHRISTMAS CAROL

(Correction of traditional misinformation)

We are Freaks

We are freaks who follow the stars,
Pleiades, Neptune, Venus and Mars;
Men and women, dressed in linen,
Peddling our lucky charms.....O

We have seen a bright new star,
Traced its track and travelled far;
From the East we've journeyed westwards-
Seeking out a baby rare!

We bring gold, a currency true,
All our wealth we offer to you;
Born in need, you have no greed,
But offer us values new......O

We have incense, sparking red,
Used by us to summon the dead;
Young life new, you bring life true,
Just as Zoroaster said…….O

We are healers of a sort,
Myrrh we use as last resort;
Ease our pain, remove the strain,
Sure healer of mind and heart…..O

You are brighter than a star,
Swarthy skin with smile so fair;
From the edge we make our pledge,
"You'll find us waiting there"…..O

Welsh Version

Ffrîcs ym ni.

Ffrîcs ym ni, sy'n dilyn y sêr,
Mawrth a Neifion a Gwener glaer;
Gwyr a gwragedd, mewn gwisg bonedd,
Gwerthwn ein swynion per……O

Gwelsom seren newydd sbon,
Yn y nen, dilynwn hon,
Taith o'r dwyrain i'r gorllewin,
Wnawn i ganfod plentyn llon.

Aur sy gennym- trysor o fri,
Ein holl gyfoeth roddwn i ti;
Tlawd yn llanc, 'rwyt heb ddim gwanc,
Tydi yw ein delfryd ni……O

Wele ein thus, yn wreichion byw
Modd i alw'r meirwon yw.
Ti yw'r Bywyd, blentyn hyfryd,
Fel d'wedodd *Soro'n wiw…….O

Dyma'n nod – yr claf i'w iachau,
Myrr ein modd, y boen i'w leihau;
Lleddfa'n poen a chym'ra'r straen,
Iachawr ein calonnau brau…….O

Tywyll dy groen a llydan dy wen,
Harddach wyt na'r sêr uwchben.
Od ym ni, ond, fel Tydi
Rhown groeso i'r rhai dan sen……..O

* h.y. Zoroaster

In Conclusion

"This is what it's like in The Bright New World. There was once a head of state whose son was getting married. The head of state was making plans for the wedding reception and sent details of the time and place to those on the invitation list. But nobody replied to say they were coming. So the head of state sent another set of messengers with a note saying, 'Everything is ready. The food has been prepared and the table decorations have been made. Please let us know if you intend to come to the wedding reception.' But nobody could be bothered to reply. One booked a holiday for the same date, another went off to a cottage in the country, and another arranged a business trip. Some gave the messengers a hostile reception. The head of state was very put out. Those who had treated the invitation with contempt were deprived of their offices of state and all their privileges. The head of state said to the messengers, 'It will all go ahead as planned, but those on the official invitation list don't deserve to be there. Go into the street

and invite everybody you meet to the wedding reception.' The messengers went up and down the high street and invited everybody, good and bad. As you can imagine, the place was heaving. But when the head of state came in to chat with the guests he noticed someone wearing a disapproving frown. The head of state said, 'Friend, how did you get in here with a face like that?' The person with the angry look couldn't think of an answer. So the bouncers were called to do their duty. The head of state said, 'Outside is the place for those who choose to be miserable.' " (God's party is for everybody, but not everybody displays the party spirit!)
(Good News from a Jewish Friend. Matthew 22)

The purpose of these studies has been to shed fresh light on our understanding of the sacred meal and its celebration. The whole atmosphere of Holy Communion undergoes a transformation the moment we begin to realise its origin is not to be found in the betrayal night alone. If that occasion of celebration is regarded as just one, perhaps the most important (perhaps not) of a series of such occasions, with hints of others, then the whole character of the meal appears significantly different from how the majority of Christians down the ages have seen it. Recently there have been moves here and there to re-instate the Agape as an alternative to Communion in some circumstances, especially in ecumenical situations where there are technical difficulties with inter-communion. Thus there is recognition that there were communal meals shared by the first Christians that were different in character from what we know as Holy Communion, and that there is need for us to repair a broken tradition. With the experience of these agape meals may come the recognition that something is amiss or missing in our more regular and stately celebrations of The Jesus Meal, which the Agape may put right by providing a supplement. This, for contemporary Christians is, as yet, new ground. For not only is there no strong drive towards frequent and wide spread agape meals among the more established denominations, but there is little in the way of theology or scriptural explanation to give meaning to such celebrations. Christians do meet together at table for what are regarded as social occasions – harvest suppers, garden parties, Mothers Union teas and the like, but not with the sense that this is central to the life and witness of the Church, but rather as time off – a relaxation, not some anxiously warn, to be indulged in too often, otherwise the churches will become too "social" and forget their prime purpose to worship God or to save souls. The harvest supper is likely to be attended by substantial numbers of people who are not seen very often at Sunday worship. Indeed, Mr. Growser will probably remark that it is a pity the prayer meeting is not so well attended. It does not occur to him to reflect that when the adventurous son returned from the far country, the appropriate celebration called for by his father was not a prayer meeting but a dinner and dance!

Supplementing the sacred meal by frequent occasions of agape, self-consciously and with theological intent labelled as such, may not be the right answer. One agape I attended lasted for over two and a half hours, during which time participants were wedged in between old-style trestle tables and obliged to listen to seven scripture readings, each followed by a substantial homily. Yet it was billed as an agape, not an agony! For the early Christians agapes were a celebration of the Supper of Jesus, the Leader, and the Supper of the Leader was an agape. It is doubtful if there was any clear distinction until the unfortunate behaviour of the Corinthians inspired Paul to suggest they do their regular eating and drinking at home. What is required is that we re-discover the agape nature of the Leader's Banquet (as Paul called it), and for this the other communions of Jesus supply the necessary scriptural and theological background. Several big shifts in emphasis will follow.

1

In the first place Holy Communion will become a more joyful event. It is the banquet of God's New World. The wedding at Cana in Galilee provides just the right picture. Thin wafers or minute crumbs of bread, followed by little sips of wine or fruit juice cannot produce the right mood. There should be plenty to eat and drink at the Leader's Banquet, to bear witness to the generosity, nay the prodigality of God's grace. As a child I wondered greatly that folk put silver coins into the collection plate that was passed round during the singing of the last hymn at communion. I felt they had been cheated. A childish misunderstanding, or was I on to something?

In traditional translations of Matthew's Gospel are recorded some words of Jesus about a 'wedding garment'. It concludes a story in which God's New World is described as a wedding feast. The nosh-up has been opened wide to all and sundry, especially sundry. It strikes us as strange that having welcomed into the feast 'good and bad alike' there is now discrimination as to clothing. The impression I was given by my spiritual mentors was that Jesus had in mind any who came to chapel not wearing their 'Sunday Best' or, if too poor to own a Sunday Best, at least 'neat and tidy'. There are pubs and clubs with notices that persons will not be admitted 'improperly or 'indecently' dressed, though what this means is not always precisely specified. Discrimination as to clothing is a smart way of eliminating undesirables. Is this sort of thing really what Jesus had in mind? 'Bible students' sometimes think it their task to work out which of the rules of church membership the erring man has broken. Has he failed to repent? Has he produced insufficient in the way of good works? Perhaps he has not been 'justified by faith', or even failed to be baptized by immersion? (Texts can always be found and put to the service of the argument.) This kind of thinking illustrates what has gone wrong with the Church in its consideration of who are worthy to join its ranks and be admitted to Holy Communion. The story is about a party and about a good time to be had by all. Who would not fit into such a picture? Only somebody who, like the elder brother, lacked the party spirit. A modern equivalent would be a fancy dress party to which someone turns up in a plain suit. They are conspicuous not because they are improper but because they are too proper. The best place for those who are determined to be miserable and spoil the fun, says Jesus, is outside the door where they may cry and grind their teeth to their heart's content. So in 'Good As New' we offer 'disapproving frown' for a contemporary equivalent of 'without a wedding garment'.

Jesus was forever off to parties, and how the strict set hated it! These parties seem to have been very open affairs. Gatecrashers had no difficulty in getting in. The strict set could get in, as they did to Matthew's party to celebrate his decision to follow Jesus. (Good News from a Jewish Friend – Matthew 9:9-13) But although they got through the door, the Pharisees excluded themselves from the feast. They could not eat because they were on a fast; they could not laugh at the cabaret because, being on a fast they were not allowed to smile; they couldn't relax in mixed company, and they were unsure whether the bathroom facilities were up to scratch. Jesus told them, "We played wedding music for you, but you wouldn't dance." "You say of me, 'Look at him, spending all his time at parties, mixing with the lowest of the low!' Intelligent folk make the right response on the right occasion." (Luke 7: 32-34)

I am grateful to my father [Fn. 4.] a saint of God if ever there was, for always refusing to take us for our family holiday to a Christian Guest House, of which there were many in days gone by – no end of 'fellowship' but sparing with the cornflakes. "When I go on holiday," he would say, "I like to be with pagans." When Christianity threw out paganism, it threw out the baby and kept the bathwater. Out went the pagan's sheer, uninhibited delight in being alive, the fitting response to God's creation of us and setting us in such a wonderful world. Carefully preserved and nourished within the Christian Church has been the pagan's enslavement to taboo and obsession with cultic detail. The pagan's love of life was something Jesus shared but which the Pharisee tragically turned away from in sorrow or envy or fear.

Let's enjoy the Banquet Jesus has invited us to – it's God's Party and should go with a swing! Well done, Mary Cotes, for introducing party poppers into our celebrations of Communion in Pontypridd!

2

The second big shift in emphasis in the celebration of the Leader's Banquet, in consequence of an examination of the other communions of Jesus, has to do with the scope of invitation to the meal. Alone of all the celebrations in Jesus' ministry, the meal on the betrayal night has some feel of a ticket-only event. Even here the seemingly exclusive nature of the meeting in the upstairs function room can be explained on the grounds of the special need for secrecy in the hour of danger, and the limits of space in the house of a sympathiser who wished to remain anonymous. Otherwise, the eating and drinking of Jesus and his friends was very public and a source of scandal. His willingness to sit at table with disreputable characters, and with lepers, was one aspect of his ministry that enflamed the hatred of his enemies and ultimately led to his death on the gallows. It is impossible to imagine, on the basis of the gospel records,

Jesus refusing to share food with anybody. He even accepted invitations to dinner from members of the strict set! In the stories to do with the Banquet of God's New World, people may exclude themselves by refusing to come to the table, or they may miss the excitement of it all by adopting negative attitudes, but no one who desires to join is excluded. The morally dubious, aliens, the theologically unorthodox, people of other faiths, are all included.

The Church has come a long way from this inclusiveness of Jesus. Until very recently, all the churches have had strict rules governing admission to Jesus' Table, and even where the rules are now relaxed a little bit, one gets the impression that this is because the decline in church membership has obliged churches to be less choosy. Still it is true that most churches expect of the communicant church membership signified by baptism and confirmation, or their equivalent, and those who do not insist on membership usually invite "all those who love the Lord" or some similar formula, which is intended as a step in the direction of the mind of Jesus, but on the basis of the other communions is still not good enough. Jesus questioned Rocky as to his love **after** communion, not before. In any case, "those who love the Lord", if taken seriously, could be a more limiting factor than church membership.

> **There is a thing that puzzles me**
> **And often gives me anxious thought;**
> **Do I love the Lord or no,**
> **Am I his or am I not?**
>
> *(Cowper)*

The logic of the Good News is that either we are all welcome to Jesus' table or none. Some will choose not to accept, either because they have no desire, or because they feel unworthy. Those who have no desire are granted freedom to refuse God's invitation (Matthew 22:3), but those who feel unworthy should be **urged** to come (Luke 14:23) since they represent the priority targeting of Jesus. Unworthiness, far from being a bar to the table, is, in the thinking of Jesus, the prime qualification. Since we are all unworthy, we should all be there.

The world, when it pays attention to the Church at all, does so with bewilderment at its self-image as a welcoming community. Those who do not belong to the Freemasons or similar exclusive part-secret societies, mistrust and resent them. To the world outside the Church seems to be a similar society, with its principle rites reserved for members (except, significantly, funerals), though spectators are allowed. Common sense would not expect the public attitude to Christians to be different from that towards any other secret society. Yet Christians remain in cuckoo-land, aggrieved because the world will not heed their message. Churches with varying degrees of enthusiasm and skill advertise their existence, if only by a notice board with the caption (unbelievable, like most adverts) "A Warm Welcome to All". Yet what would we think of someone who gave us a warm invitation to their home and then, having seated us on uncomfortable and unsociable seating, proceeded to lecture us on their view of the truth and to put loaded words into our hands for us to recite and sing in time with them, and then, after a prayer for our forgiveness, when the time for refreshments comes, assure us there is no need for us to go – we can stay and watch, or even, if we wish, approach the table and receive a blessing!?

Side by side with this strange behaviour vis à vis the respectable folk the churches are eager to draw within their ranks (gifted people able to help with the 'work'), must be placed its even more strange behaviour vis à vis the less respectable members of society Jesus was so concerned about. There are some churches in our inner city areas, and other areas where there is visible deprivation, which conduct a special ministry to the hungry homeless. My own church in Pontypridd was one such church until recently, when the local authority provided alternative accommodation to the night-shelter we housed. Such work is vital, an expression of the compassion of Jesus, and would that more churches were aware of the problem and willing to make the necessary sacrifices to get involved. But, all too often, the pattern is that, in one section of the church premises meets the well dressed congregation who celebrate Holy Communion in an orderly and seemly fashion, whereas in another section of the premises meet the smelly, unkempt types who arrive for their warm-up and refreshments. The work done in this room is done in the name of the people upstairs or next-door. These contribute financially, some even lending a hand. Yet what a bizarre denial of the banquet of God's New World is demonstrated by this separation. It is not only that two groups of needy people are divided by social class as they come to be fed in the name of Jesus, but that what is going on in one place is thought of as being the central event of the church, and what is going on in the other place is thought of as peripheral to it. Holy Communion, the banquet of God's New World, is celebrated fittingly when these two congregations eat and drink together, otherwise it is the fringe celebration that is closer to what Jesus had in mind when he called his people to eat and drink in his memory.

Just down the road from where I live, there is a large Baptist Church that provides a Christmas meal on its premises for those not likely to get one otherwise. That occasion should be looked upon as the High Mass of the year, the true celebration of God Incarnate, the Word made flesh, not just a kind and thoughtful piece of social work. For those church members who give up their Christmas meal at home to be present at this communion it is a privilege beyond all other to be present with Jesus at his table and to wait upon and celebrate with his favourite people.

Some churches are much exercised in mind as to whether children should be allowed to partake of the bread and wine, though in some churches the question does not even arise since it is assumed that children have no place at Jesus' table. In some churches, even today, care is taken to make sure they are not even present, lest they spoil the atmosphere. Where the debate is taking place, it centres on theological considerations, such as whether the element of commitment, undoubtedly an important aspect of Communion as traditionally understood, is essential to participation. When, however, we turn our attention to the other communions of Jesus, the answer comes quite simply and we can stop flapping. Children were present at the feeding of the five thousand. They are purposefully mentioned as being present and eating. (Matthew 14:21) And if it is argued that this was because they were members of the covenant people, not so the children who are mentioned with the four thousand who, more likely than not, were Gentiles. (Matthew 15:33) According to 'Sources Close to Jesus' (John's Gospel), it was a young lad who supplied the five loaves and two fishes – the hero of Sunday School days, conveniently forgotten in our adult arguments. (John 6:9) So let the children come and eat from Jesus' table, the only doubt being whether bread and wine are sufficiently exciting for a child – about as exciting as the paste sandwiches provided on Sunday School outings in days remembered. Imagination is required when providing for children, which is why they are so good for the Church, these ex-officio members of God's New World. (Mark 10:15) Although the sweets and chocolate I put on the communion plates with the bread are meant for the children (sugar eggs and chocolate fish at Easter), I have learnt to provide enough for the adults.

One of the chief objections to children sharing communion is that they will not understand what they are doing. This, on the one hand, expresses adult arrogance, and on the other, an admission that our provision for Christian education is not up to much. Every participant understands the meal in their own way and distinctions or levels of understanding have little to do with the child/adult divide. However, the celebration of Holy Communion is not primarily a matter of understanding, but of doing. We all know how to eat and drink, whereas we do not all know how to express ourselves verbally or appreciate lofty sermons. That is why the sacrament is, or should be, such a uniting force. Those who have reflected for many years on the deep things of the faith can join at Jesus' Table with those who know next to nothing, and be at one.

3

Lastly, study of the other communions of Jesus should lead to an expansion of the menu for Holy Communion. Coming after the points just made about the recapture of joy for the festal meal and maximum inclusiveness, talk of menu may seem frivolous. Yet all these things are bound up together. Diversity in the food offered at the altar symbolizes the diversity in humankind. A move away from sparse rations speaks of the abundant life in which receivers of the Good News rejoice. The simple communion of bread and wine will remain part of the overall round of celebration, for it has been imprinted deep in the spiritual consciousness of the people of God for most of their history. It speaks of the essential simplicity of our faith, and of our involvement together with God in the sufferings and deprivations of the world. But there should be other times when the table overflows – the same table, the same people, the same faith. Jesus, when he called his friends to eat and drink in memory of him, surely did not expect them to do so always on a starvation diet. Wedding guests don't fast! (Mark 2:19) Even the sad communion in the function room upstairs, was a full meal with an elaborate, time-honoured menu, though appetites were restrained by the tense and gloomy atmosphere. Attention to the other communions of Jesus makes us aware that fish was an element almost as often as bread and more often than wine. So that limiting the menu to bread and wine cannot be regarded as scriptural. Bread and wine and fish, also spring water and honey, are all elements in scripture loaded with symbolism. They can be used time and time again to teach the truths of the Good News. Other forms of good food and drink can speak of God's loving provision too. The God pictured by Jesus in the story of the Wedding celebrations, is a jovial soul, heartily chuffed as guests behold, wide-eyed, the expanse and variety of the food placed before them. Indeed, the powerful gospel symbol of the banquet can only be fully realized when a banquet is provided. Occasions where the Christian community already feasts can be used as the starting point for these communions – the harvest supper, the Easter breakfast, the Christmas Eve or New Year's Eve social. Also occasions of family celebration – weddings and christenings, where church catering facilities are made available and church members act in their proper role as servers. Communion accompanying the reception of new members into the Christian community should be of this kind. Also that to celebrate the welcome given to those who transfer from one local church to another. At the very least there should be a cake or trifle presented at Jesus' table to be shared as part of the celebration to follow, provided by the new members, their sponsors or their friends. The call of Matthew (Matthew 9:9) or Keith (Zaccheus) (Luke 19) are suitable readings for such occasions.

I now refrain from offering any further practical suggestions. I would rather Christian communities work out the principles derived from these studies themselves, with imagination and daring. The greater the variety, the greater the sense of novelty and surprise, the better, for these are all factors associated with celebration. As long as the presence of the risen Jesus is recognized and his Good News proclaimed, for he is both host and guest of honour whenever his people meet to eat and drink.

I remember on one occasion eating out with a friend in a restaurant, when there was a sudden stir among the staff. An inconspicuous little man had come in and sat down at one of the tables. Suddenly the quality of the service improved markedly. The waiters became twice as nimble on their feet and anxious to please, and it was possible to sense vibrations signifying near panic from the direction of the kitchen. The helpings of the sweet also seemed to be slightly larger than usual. The owner of the chain of restaurants of which this restaurant was one, had made an unscheduled appearance. What does Jesus think of the performance of his staff as they wait at his table, and what is his opinion of the fare?

JESUS INVITES US ALL

Jesus invites us all
To come and gather round;
Here, for whoever wants a meal,
A welcome will be found.

Some simple food and drink
Will give the signs we need
To know our friend once died for us,
And now is risen indeed.

As here on earth, love spoke
In everything he did;
Love speaks again in broken crusts,
And as the cup is shared.

Each of us different from
The person sitting near,-
Jesus breaks all the barriers down
And overcomes our fear.

So now we lift our hearts,
Feelings and voices raise;
Jesus requests our company;
Let's shower him with praise!

(After Isaac Watts 'Jesus invites his saints' tune: Bod Alwyn)

[Fn.4.] The Revd. W. Clifford Henson, late of Magor, Gwent, who was a Baptist minister with pastorates in South Wales and the West Country of England.

APPENDIX ONE

COMMUNION AT CANA IN GALILEE

(Suitable for New Year, Epiphany and Pre-Lent)

Scripture Sentence: *'..eat your bread with enjoyment and drink your wine with a merry heart; for God has long ago approved what you do.'* (Ecclesiates 9: 7 NRSV)

Hymn 'Deck yourselves with joy and gladness' (As in chapter one)

Prayer: God of joy and high spirits; God of laughter and fun; we accept your invitation to eat and drink with you; we come to enjoy the life you offer us in Jesus – a life packed with good things. Make our joy deep, real, and lasting, rooted in your perfect love for us. Amen.

Readings: **Hebrew Scriptures:** 2 Kings 2: 19-22 **or** 1 Kings 17: 8-16 **or** Jeremiah 31: 29-34

Psalm 104

Early Christian Scriptures: Good News from Sources Close to Jesus 2: 1-11 (Good As New)

Post Biblical Scriptures: (Make a choice in the spirit of the subject from a favourite Christian writer)

e.g. Herbert Butterfield- Christianity and History 1950, Concluding thoughts.

'In regard to some of the most important things in life it is remarkable how little human beings know of their liberty- how little they realise that the grand discoveries of the sciences still leave us free to range with the upper parts of our minds. In these days also when people are so much the prisoners of systems, it is not always realised that belief in God gives us greater elasticity of mind. If one wants a permanent rock in life and goes deep enough for it, it is difficult for historical events to shake it. We can do worse than remember a principle which both gives us a firm Rock and leaves us the maximum elasticity for our minds: the principle: Hold to Christ, and for the rest be totally uncommitted.' (Slightly abbreviated)

(Optional) **Bidding:** Give thanks for every way God speaks to us **Response:** We thank you, God.

Prayer: Loving Friend, we express our concern to you for those who do not yet share your joy, and others who may have lost it: the poor in material wealth, and the poor in spirit; the lonely and the shy; the sad and the disappointed; the depressed and the frustrated; the bitter and the cold-hearted. Let them hear, through us, your invitation to the Banquet of your New World, to your community of love and peace. (Specific requests may be added)

Traditional Hymn: Thy ceaseless, unexhausted love (Wesley)

The Meal. (Words based on the Living Bible and Good As New)

L. Jesus' mother was a guest at a wedding in the village of Cana in Galilee, and Jesus and his friends were invited too. Jesus is here!

***R.* His Spirit is with us!**

L. The bridegroom has come!

***All.* Let the festivities begin!**

L. He brings his Peace.

***All.* Let us share it with one another.** (Guests greet one another affectionately)

(Leader takes bread and/or wedding cake)

L. Let's ask God to make these gifts a source of happiness.

Al: **God, use these gifts to our delight and help us to be your friends.**

(Bread or wedding cake is broken and handed round)

L. They ran out of drinks during the party, and Jesus' mother came to him with the problem. She told the waiters, "Do whatever he tells you." Jesus said to the waiters, "Go to the well and take what you draw from it to the master of ceremonies."

(A cup of water is handed round)

L. When the master of ceremonies tasted the drink from the well, he called across to the bridegroom, "This is wonderful stuff! You've kept the best till last!"

(Wine, fruit juice or sparkling drink is handed round)

L. Whenever we eat or drink together, we are in company with Jesus, the life and soul of the party.

All: Loving God, here and everywhere, help us proclaim your values and bring in your New World. Supply us our day-to-day needs. Forgive us for wounding you, while we forgive those who wound us. Give us courage to meet life's trials and deal with evil's power. We celebrate your New World, full of life and beauty, lasting for ever. **(The Pattern Prayer)**

Hymn: Father, who in Jesus found us (Fred Kaan)

All: **The beauty of Jesus our Leader. The love of God our Parent, and the joy of the Spirit our uniter be with us for ever.**

Additional Prayers.

A. God of love, origin and inspiration of every loving relationship, we pray for those who today experience the bliss of mutual affection. May the excitement and thrill of heart beating with heart issue in the strength and comfort of a shared life and a common care for each other's needs. Especially we pray for those who at this time are entering into a relationship of special commitment, celebrated in your presence and in the presence of other people. May joy and a sense of responsibility go hand in hand; may divine ecstasy give meaning and sense to the trivial and the ordinary. Save all lovers from the twin enemies of jealousy and possessiveness, that other friends may share the cup that overflows. And for those still looking for human love, or who are injured by its loss, let them know the assurance of your everlasting love, which passes all knowledge.

B. God, you made your home with us in Jesus. We pray for all homes and families where people are bound together by special ties of flesh and blood. We pray for parents and children, that they may care about one another's needs rather than false rights of ownership. For adolescents recklessly breaking free or too timid to break free. And for adults having to adjust to their children's freedom and their own, we pray for courage and sensitivity. For mothers, like Mary the mother of Jesus, coping as the only parent of a family, and for fathers in a similar position, we pray for special gifts to be both father and mother. When quarrels arise may they be swiftly brought to an end in forgiveness and acceptance and a more mature understanding. May parents and children, brothers and sisters, experience the added joy of becoming friends. We ask these things as friends of Jesus.

C. God of all, we thank you for the New Covenant Jesus brought about: for this new relationship with you based not on rules and regulations or on fear of your displeasure, but on the love you made known in him. Thank you that in Jesus we are free to grow towards you, assured of your encouragement and understanding every step of the way: no longer working out our guilt in intolerance and aggressiveness towards others: no longer seeking to justify or explain ourselves. Help us not to fall back into old dark ways, to lose the freedom won for us by Jesus. Help us to cut the chains that bind other people and lead them into the light at a pace they can manage. Open our eyes to the banquet you have spread before us: Let us make merry at your Good News.

(Optional) Bidding: **Loving God** Response: **Use our prayer**

APPENDIX TWO

COMMUNION AT THE WELL

(Suitable for Lent)

Scripture Sentence: Jesus shouted out, "Anyone who is thirsty can come to me for a drink. Whoever trusts me will have a supply of fresh water inside them." (Sources close to Jesus 7: 37-38)

Hymn: I heard the voice of Jesus say (Horatius Bonar)

Prayer: God, friend and lover of all, we encounter you in the friendship that arises from need. You have said that you need us, though we are amazed that this should be so. You seek our company and our heart's affections, and ask us to do things for you.

We need you. Although you have made us, we are free to go our own way. Yet nothing makes sense without you, and we believe that you alone can satisfy our deepest longings and sort out our frustrations. Meet us now at this resting place on life's journey; talk with us as with your people long ago; offer us the water of life and the food of eternal wholeness. And ask of us what you will. In Jesus we have seen your love in a person.

Readings:

Hebrew Scriptures **Isaiah 55**

Psalm 42

Early Christian Scriptures **Sources 4: 1-25**

Post-Biblical Scripture **e.g.**

'We are to be centres through which Jesus can flow as rivers of living water in blessing to everyone. Some of us are like the Dead Sea. Always taking in but never giving out, because we are not rightly related to the Lord Jesus. Keep at the Source, guard well your belief in Jesus Christ and your relationship to him, and there will be a steady flow for other lives, no dryness and no deadness.

Is it not too extravagant to say that out of an individual believer, rivers are going to flow? 'I do not see rivers', you say. Never look at yourself from the standpoint of- "Who am I?" In the history of God's work you will nearly always find that it has started from the obscure, the unknown, the ignored, but the steadfastly true to Jesus Christ.' (Oswald Chambers comment for September 7th 'My

Utmost for His Highest 1927)

(Optional) Bidding: **Praise God who speaks to us**
Response: **Praise God!**

Hymn: **There's a spirit in the air (Brian Wren)**

The Meal
(Voices: Narrator, Woman, Jesus, All)

N: Jesus decided to go through Samaria. He came to a village called Jacob's Well. The well was still there. Jesus was feeling tired after the hard walk, so he sat down by the well. A woman from the village came to get some water, and Jesus said to her,

J: Give me a drink

W: How can you, a Jew, ask me for a drink? I'm a woman, and what's more, born and bred here in Samaria!

N: Jews do not eat or drink with people from Samaria.

J: If only you knew what God has on offer and who is saying to you, 'Give me a drink', *you* would be the one to ask, and I would provide you with a constant supply of water. Whoever drinks water from this well will be thirsty again, but those who drink the water I give them will never be thirsty. The water I give them will turn into a spring of water deep inside them and give life to the full.

All: Give me that water.

Cup/s of sparkling mineral water passed around)

J: The time's coming, has come in fact, when people seeking to worship the Loving God will worship with sincerity of heart and mind. God's Spirit is like the wind, open and free. God's worshipers must be the same.

N: Jesus' friends had gone to the village to buy food. When they came back they were surprised to find him chatting with a woman. Then the woman left her water jar and went back to the village. Meanwhile Jesus' friends tried to get him to eat something. But Jesus said,

J: I've got food to eat you don't know anything about.

(A hamper is opened containing a variety of food. Suggestions: small cakes [especially currant cakes, Welsh cakes etc], fruit [grapes, dates, figs, pomegranate segments, nuts] oriental spice mix. Food is distributed.)

J: My food is to please the one who sent me and to finish the job I've been given.

Prayer: Jesus, friend of outcasts and offenders, yourself despised and rejected by the society of your day, we pray for all who have been pushed to the margins of life, those who are or feel themselves to be persecuted: For those whose religion, cultural background, sex, personality, past history or point of view results in isolation, on their own or in the insecurity of ghettos:

Bidding: Loving God **Response:** Hold them in your arms

For prisoners of conscience and for prisoners who have no conscience but who suffer just the same: For those who long for things to be different, and for those who have given up longing: For those who are regarded as evil and a threat though they are not, and for those who really are evil and seek only to injure and destroy: That all may be dealt with according to your principles of justice and truth.

Bidding: Loving God **Response:** Hold them in your arms

We pray for those whose pattern of life conforms to the expectations of society, those who obey the rules, achieve their goals and cause no obvious trouble. We pray that they may be sensitive and understanding of those who find life difficult and are not able to conform; that their peace may be disturbed, if necessary, to bring peace to others.

Bidding: Loving God **Response:** Hold them in your arms

Pattern Prayer (See Appendix One)

Hymn When the church of Jesus (Pratt Green) and/or Go forth and tell (James Seddon) (Why not sing two hymns one after the other? The first of these may be sung seated, the second requires standing!)

Passing on the Goodness (Blessing) God cheer you and look after you; God convince you that life is good; God assure you that love is the lasting reality; God satisfy your deepest needs; God give you peace, now and for ever.

APPENDIX THREE

COMMUNION IN THE CORNFIELD

(Suitable for Summertime)

Scripture God says, "I would feed you with the finest of the wheat, and with honey from the rock I would satisfy you." (Psalm 81 NRSV)

Hymn Come with me, come wander (Bell and Maule- Iona Community)

Prayer God of freedom; help us to be ourselves in your company. God of peace; help us to relax in your presence; God of celebration; help us to rejoice with you; God of delight; help us to thrill at the feast you have prepared for us. God of comfort; take away all fears and sorrow. God of forgiveness; take away all bitterness and resentment. God of love; teach us to love with your love.

Readings

Hebrew Scriptures 1 Samuel 21: 1-6

Early Christian Scriptures Mark 2: 23-28

Post-Biblical Scriptures e.g. Leonardo Boff

'Jesus never used the word "Obedience". The preaching and demands of Christ do not presuppose an established order. Rather, on the contrary, he frustrates it because of his creative imagination and spontaneity. We do not mean to say that Jesus made no harsh demands. Obedience for him is not a question of fulfilling orders, but a firm decision in favor of what God demands within a concrete situation.

The great difficulty encountered by Jesus in his disputes with theologians and masters of his time consisted in precisely this: We cannot resolve the question what God wants from us by merely having recourse to the scriptures. Obedience is a question of having our eyes open to the situation: it consists in deciding for and risking ourselves in the adventure of responding to God who speaks here and now. The Sermon on the Mount, which is not law, is addressed to everyone, inviting us to have extremely clear consciences and an unlimited capacity for understanding people, sympathizing with them, being tuned into them, and loving them with all their limitations.' (Jesus Christ Liberator. Chapter: Jesus, a Person of Extraordinary Good Sense, Creative Imagination, and Originality.)

Hymn The Kingdom of God is justice and joy (Bryn Austin Rees)

The Meal

Leader: One Rest Day, Jesus and his friends were going for a walk through the cornfields. As they went along, they began to pluck the ears of corn.

(Leader displays a plate of puffed wheat, pop corn, or small cakes made with honey(or chocolate) and puffed wheat or rice crispies.)

Let us thank God for providing us with food.

***All*:** You are source of all happiness, our God, Ruler of the Universe. You feed the whole world with your kindness and love. You make ample provision for all: your generosity flows on and on for ever. Through your great goodness, we have never lacked food: may it never fail us, for the sake of your great name. For you nourish and sustain all beings and all benefit from what you do for them. All living things are alive with your life and you attend to their needs. Source of all happiness, God, the one who gives food to all, we present our thankful hearts to you. (After a Jewish grace.)

(The food is shared)

Leader: Jesus said, "Anyone used to drinking vintage wine will not be enthusiastic about cheap table wine." He also said, "You don't put new wine into dirty old bottles. You'd ruin the wine that way!" (Good As New 'Thought-Provoking Sayings')

(Leader displays a tray with a choice of drinks- fruit juice, mineral water, tonic water, wine).

Jesus said: "I'm the grapevine, you're the branches. If we stay attached to one another there'll be a good crop."

(The drinks are shared)

Leader: A man said to Jesus, "It seems to me there are many standing round the bar waiting for a drink, but the tap's run dry!" Jesus said, "I'd put it another way. At a party there are always some who nervously huddle together near the door, but only those who take that lonely step and walk right in enjoy the fun!" (Thought-Provoking Sayings)

Prayer: Dear God, thankyou for your amazing world, full of interest, delight, and surprises too. Thank you that there is usually enough to occupy us and to satisfy our curiosity, though it never seems enough when our appetites are out of control and our desires insatiable. Give us the cheerful heart that tastes your gifts with joy and the imaginative mind that finds the new and exciting even in the old and familiar. When we go on a walk may we find ourselves with you and your first friends, strolling through the fields or by the lakeside, on the rough road from Jerusalem to Jericho or through the busy markets and temple precincts. May the landscape and the wildlife, the shoppers and the traders, the fisherfolk and the lawyers, the police and the clergy still speak to us your truths as they did in the days of old, not just old truths, but the new truths you always have on offer for us as soon as we are ready. Save us from being so serious and pious that, like the Pharisees, we take all the fun and enjoyment out of life, spoiling things for ourselves and for others. Teach us the joy that is encouragement and kindness in disguise and makes everybody feel better. Help us to log on to the comfort that soothes and heals even the sharpest pains and turns bitterness into quiet acceptance, and finally into energy for positive good and help for others.

We pray for the bored, the frustrated, those who have lost interest and ignore the opportunities and avenues for friendship. For those who complain that the tap has run dry, and who lack the will to go to the party. For those who can only see the nasty, unpleasant and dangerous aspects of life, and who dedicate themselves to judgement and warning, instead of helping and inspiring. For those who have fallen down and will not let anyone help them to their feet. For those who aim to squeeze the very last drop out of life, then suddenly are surprised to find there is no more left. For those who have joy and a merry spirit but are in danger of losing it because they are becoming selfish and careless. For all of us, that those things which are destructive and selfish and negative within us may not get the upper hand, but be overcome by the love which God seeks to share with us by means of Jesus, the friend of all.

Together: Teach us Jesus, to help you all we can; to give without resentment more than we intended; to love and accept love and cope with its pain; to enjoy work, rest and play; to be friends you can rely on; for your sake and ours. (After Ignatius Loyola)

Hymn

THE SHARP WINDS OF CHANGE

The sharp winds of change are now sweeping our land-
It's you, God, we recognize your Spirit's hand;
She's waking our dull, unadventurous faith,
And nothing is certain or rigid or safe.

Welcome God, welcome new, welcome Spirit again;
In your life, in your love, never one day the same;
We join, as your family, to work and adore,
Your great world to care for, enjoy and explore.

We thank you for leading us right where we are,
For giving the courage to do and to dare,
For lifting our hearts when our feelings were low,
Your laughter to echo, your beauty to show.

Through many a torment and many an ill,
You've led us through valley and over the hill,
We've marked pleasant vistas and frightening scenes,
But the country we long for will outshine our dreams.

Today you are with us, inspiring our song,
You bind us together to know we belong;
We welcome the sharp winds, disturbing our ways,
Sure sign of your Spirit, God- yours be the praise!

(Inspired by John Gwilym Jones 'Fe chwythodd yr awel..' and the tune 'To God be the glory' W.H.Doane

APPENDIX FOUR

PICNIC COMMUNION ON THE GRASS

Scripture: *'The God of love* lets me rest in fields of green grass and leads me to quiet pools of fresh water.
You prepare a banquet for me, where all my enemies can see me; you welcome me as an honoured guest and fill my cup to the brim.' (Psalm 23 GNB)

Hymn

IT'S VERY RARE

It's very rare to work for God,
To stand and take God's part
In this confusing, anxious world,
And not sometimes lose heart.

The God of Love plays hide and seek,
Or so it often seems;
The New World frequently recedes
Way off beyond our dreams.

Playmates of God, just try again;
Search the unlikely spot;
Your dearest friend is teasing you,
Just waiting to be caught.

You'll be at ease when you just trust
Your instinct, which can tell
That God is, like a summer breeze,
Warm though invisible.

It's hard to know what's right from wrong;
To question we are free;
To doubt is not disloyalty;
Love always holds the key.

You're feeling down? - you've joined the saints-
They know just how you feel.
Come, rest awhile, and shed your load;
The hidden one will heal.

(After F.W. Faber 1814-63)

Prayer: God, you are the source of our desire. You have put longings in our hearts and minds so that we seek and strive and aspire. We know we are not complete; we know we have not attained our full potential; we sense we have a destiny. Be our guide as we seek our goal: be our food as we seek to alleviate our hunger and thirst: be our life as we seek fulfilment. Let your gracious gifts be our joy and a call to praise: and let each experience of what is good and pleasant be a taster of the lasting satisfaction to be found in you.

Scripture Readings: Hebrew Scriptures Exodus 16: 1-15 Psalm 107: 1-9

Early Christian Scriptures: 'From a Jewish Friend' 14: 13-21 or 'Sources' 6: 25-51 (Good As New)

Post-Biblical Scriptures: 'Every Good and Perfect Gift' – SorenKierkegaard.

' "Every good and perfect gift is from above". These words are again and again repeated in the world, and yet many go on as if they had never heard them, and it would perhaps have affected them disturbingly if they had heard them. Carelessly they go on their way, a friendly fate makes everything so easy for them, every wish is fulfilled, all their undertakings are successful. Without knowing how it comes about, they are in the midst of the life movement, a link in the chain which connects a future with a past. Unconcerned about how it happened they are borne along on the wave of the present. That there are good and perfect gifts they know well; they also know where these come from; for the earth gives its increase, and heaven sends the early and the late rain, and family and friends consider it best for them; and their plans, wise and intelligent, succeed as is natural since they are wise and intelligent. For them life holds no riddle, and yet their life is a riddle, a dream… They let their thought for a moment occupy itself with the words, and then they said, "Now we have understood them, bring us some new thoughts which we have not

understood." Nor would they have been wrong; for the apostle's words are not difficult. And yet they proved, in that having understood the words they wished to abandon them, that they had ***not*** *understood them.'* (*Edifying discourses)*

Prayer: Kind God, we pray for all those who find it difficult to appreciate your gifts. Those the sun's rays provide no cheer for, the songs of the birds no melody, the taste of food no sweetness. We pray for those deprived of what all people should have in terms of shelter, food, clothing and companionship. For those who yearn for what they cannot have; for those who believe they have missed their opportunities; for those whose desires and ambitions are such that they only cause trouble and frustration. We pray for those whose natural affections have been twisted into something ugly and dangerous, and for those whose desires are their tyrants rather than their inspiration. We pray that none may give up hope, that none may despair of finding their heart's desire, and that all may rest in the knowledge that they have been made for you and that your love has a purpose for them.

Traditional Hymn My God I thank thee who has made (Adelaide Anne Procter) or My heart is resting, O my God (Anna Laetitia Waring)

The Meal
(Voices: Presider, 1st Voice, 2ns Voice)

1st Voice: Jesus said, "Let's go somewhere quiet and have a rest for a while"

(Moment of silence)

2nd Voice: As he got out of the boat, Jesus saw a big crowd and was deeply sorry for them. They looked lost.

(Silence)

Presider: Jesus said, "How many loaves have you got? Go and find out!"

(A search is made of the congregation. Either (i) Each member of the congregation who is asked shrugs their shoulders. Then a child, or the youngest, comes forward with the five loaves [unleavened] and the two fish in a basket- real fish (whitebait) or chocolate fish. Others from the congregation who have been hiding their food now bring it forward- e.g. Garibaldi biscuits, fig rolls, date cake etc!) Or (ii) Five members of the congregation have one loaf each, and two have the real or representative fish. Some offer their food willingly, others do so under protest.

Presider: They said,
***All*:** We have found five loaves and two fish.

(The food is put on plates. Period of silence)

2nd Voice: Jesus took the loaves and the fish, and said "thankyou" to God.

Presider: Thank you God for food; for the pleasure of tasting and the good feeling of hunger satisfied. Thankyou for the joy of eating in company and the delight of sharing.

Feed us and all who hunger, now and always, with yourself, given to us in Jesus.

1st Voice: Jesus broke the loaves and gave them to his friends to hand round to the people – men women and children.

(Bread is broken and handed round)

2nd Voice: Jesus also divided the fish among them.

(Fish and/or other food handed round)

President: Everyone had enough to eat. The leftovers filled twelve baskets.

(**An offering is taken for those in need**)

Pattern Prayer: Loving God, here and everywhere, help us proclaim your values and bring in your New World. Supply us our day to day needs. Forgive us for wounding you, while we forgive those who wound us. Give us courage to meet life's trials and deal with evil's power. We celebrate your New World, full of life and beauty, lasting forever.

Hymn Almighty Father, who for us thy Son didst give (George Caird)

Passing on the Goodness: God cheer you and look after you; God convince you that life is good; God assure you that love is the lasting reality; God satisfy your deepest needs; God give you peace, now and for ever.

APPENDIX FIVE

COMMUNION AT THE EDGE

(Suitable for Summer time)

Scripture Sentence: *'Jesus has brought us into the family of God through trust. All of you who declared your trust in Jesus share his identity. Difference of origin, sex, and class no longer matter. You all belong to one another because you belong to Jesus.'* (Paul's letter to some Celtic Christians 3: 26-28. Galatians)

Hymn: Christ is the world's true light, *the bringer* of salvation (G.W. Briggs)

Prayer: God, our eternal father and mother, all are included in your invitation to share your gifts. No one is excluded from your love. We praise you for your wide open arms displayed for us in Jesus; for your acceptance of those the world and Church reject; for your understanding when men and women refuse to understand; and for your compassion and forgiveness when the righteous seek to condemn and punish. We pray for your Spirit, that by her we may be inspired to true worship, where our songs of thanksgiving spill over into deeds of kindness and courage.

Scripture Readings: Hebrew Scriptures Jonah chapters 4 and 5 or Isaiah 49: 5-7 (Not GNB since here it misses the point).

Psalm 23

Early Christian Scriptures Good As New 'A Circular Letter' 2: 11-22

Post Biblical Scripture

'I say to you today, my friends, that in spite of the difficulties and frustrations of the moment I still have a dream…I have a dream that one day this nation will rise up and live out the true meaning of its creed: "We hold these truths to be self-evident; that all men are created equal."…. I have a dream that my four little children will one day live in a nation where they will not be judged by the color of their skin but by the content of their character. ***I have a dream today.***

I have a dream that one day every valley shall be exalted, every hill and mountain shall be made low, the rough places will be made plains, and the crooked places will be made straight, and the glory of the Lord shall be revealed, and all flesh shall see it together…

When we let freedom ring, when we let it ring from every village and every hamlet, from every state and every city, we will be able to speed up that day when all of God's children, black and white, Jews and Gentiles, Protestants and Catholics, will be able to join hands and sing in the words of that old Negro spiritual, "Free at last! Free at last! Thank God almighty, we are free at last!" (From 'I have a Dream' Speech of Martin Luther King, Washington D.D. August 28, 1963)

Prayers: Loving God, we present before you with concern all those people in the world who feel rejected or misunderstood.

Bidding: Open hearted God **Response:** We open our hearts.

We pray for those who have failed in the game of 'getting on', who have been unable to impress others by their talents or achievements, or by their good behaviour.

Bidding: Open hearted God **Response:** We open our hearts.

We pray for those marginalized into unhealthy and unhappy ghettos, or their own private shells, insecure and threatened. We think of those who feel obliged to apologize for their very existence, so little are they valued or appreciated.

Bidding: Open hearted God **Response:** Teach us to embrace like you.

We ask that we may be instruments in bringing dignity and hope to all people, but especially to those who need it most. Help us to search the highways and byways of the world with imagination and sensitivity, and never to rest until your redeeming love has reached all.

We pray for…(here there may be prayers for any specific groups or individuals)

Bidding: Loving God **Response:** Hold them in your arms

Hymn Let there be light, let there be understanding (Wheeler Davies)

The Meal (Readers: Narrator; Jesus; Disciples(All)

ALL STAND

Narrator: 'It was during a visit abroad that Jesus again found himself with a large crowd of hungry people. Jesus called his friends together and said,

Jesus: I'm concerned about all these people who've been with me for three days and haven't eaten. If I send them away hungry, some may collapse before they get home, because they've come a long way.

Disciples: How can we get enough food to feed everyone, out here in the country?
Jesus: How many loaves have you got?

Disciples: Seven

(Seven bread rolls are presented)

Narrator: Jesus told the crowd to sit down

ALL SIT

Then Jesus took the seven loaves and said 'thank you' to God.

Prayer of Thanksgiving for the Bread. (All)

God we thank you for providing us with enough for our needs and more. Help us to feed your hungry children from your abundance. We thank you your supplies never run short. Jesus is the bread of life for the whole world. As we find our personal satisfaction in him, may we yet remain dissatisfied until all are fed.

Narrator: Jesus broke the loaves and gave them to his friends to pass among the crowd.

(Each comes to the table, takes a piece of bread, then hands it to someone else. When all have bread, all eat together)

Disciples: We also have a few small fish.

(Fish are presented. Also grapes may be presented at this point)

Narrator: Jesus gave thanks for the fish.

Prayer of Thanksgiving for the Fish. (All)

Jesus, God's true Likeness, bringer of life, we thank you for this sign. You shared fish with your friends before and after your rising from the dead. You taught them to fish for men and women. So may we share your new life and your responsibilities.

Narrator: Jesus handed on the fish to be passed round.

(Some friends take the fish around; others the grapes. There may also be other food and drink on offer. All make their choice and eat at leisure)

Narrator: The crowd had as much to eat as they wanted and the leftovers were collected

(A *freewill* collection may be made of money or objects that people have on them or for which they may write an I.O.U. Or *all* may be given a scrap of paper on which they may write an intention to give something extra to somebody or do something extra for somebody in the near future.)

Scripture Sentences*:* *Jesus said: " People will come down the wide roads from every part of the world to be at the big party to celebrate God's New World. Those now thought of as no-hopers will have the best seats, whereas those who think they deserve special status will be lucky to get a seat at all."* (Luke 13: 29 & 30)

Hymn Son of God, eternal Saviour (S.C.Lowry)

Bidding: Peace be with you **Response:** And with you too.

(All give one another signs of affection)

APPENDIX SIX

EASTER DAY EVENING

Scripture Sentence: ' "Leader, when did we ever give you a good meal or stand you a drink? When did we have you in our house or give you clothes? We don't remember you being ill or visiting you in prison." Then the Leader will say, "Believe me, when you did these things for people most think not worth the trouble, you did them for me. They are my family." (Good News from a Jewish Friend. Chapter 25:37)

Hymn

HE IS ALIVE! TIME TO REJOICE

He is alive! Time to rejoice;
Now is the day to find your voice;
Tell every culture, every creed,
"The one you seek is risen indeed!"

He is alive! Who then shall fear
To face life's challenges are care?
Or make their feelings truly known
To him who craves no crown or throne?

He is alive! The verdict stands.
You are set free by nail-pierced hands;
Justice more kind that courts decide-
A judge who takes the offender's side!

He is alive! The barriers fall;
The Holy City welcomes all;
Villains and victims, straight and queer,
All now to one another dear.

One world – a dream beyond all hope,
Jesus has brought within our scope.
You know his love, you know his name;
So sing along and spread his fame!

(After Josiah Conder 'The Lord is King! Lift up thy voice.')

Prayer: Jesus, as on the first Easter Day you visited your friends, in ones and twos and together, to cheer them up and renew their confidence, so we anticipate your meeting with us this evening, to encourage and equip some of your twenty-first century friends. The table we have set is your table, waiting for you. We need to set aside our reservations, so that we can make you welcome. Open our eyes and alert all our senses to recognize you when you greet us.

Readings:

Hebrew Scriptures Genesis 18: 1-15

Early Christian Scriptures Luke 24: 13-43

Post-Biblical Scriptures e.g.

'God is the perfect friend. So that there should be between God and us, bridging the infinite distance, something in the way of equality. God has chosen to place an absolute quality on creatures, the absolute liberty of consent, which leaves us free to follow or swerve from the God-ward direction God has communicated to our souls. God has also extended our possibilities of error and falsehood so as to leave us the faculty of exercising a spurious rule in imagination, not only over the universe and the human race, but also over God, in so far as we do not know how to use God's name aright. God has given us this faculty of infinite illusion so that we should have the power to renounce it out of love.

In fact, contact with God is the true sacrament.

We can, however, be almost certain that those, whose love of God has caused the disappearance of the pure loves belonging to our life here below, are no true friends of God.

Our neighbours, our friends, religious ceremonies and the beauty of the world do not fall to the level of unrealities after the soul has had contact with God. On the contrary, it is only then that these things become real. Previously they were half dreams. Previously there was no reality.' (from Simone Weil 'Waiting on God' 1950)

Prayers: (**Bidding:** Jesus, friend of everybody
Response: Draw near to them.)

Let us pray:

1) For the homeless. For those driven from their homes by famine, war or political change; for those who are unhoused due to the inadequacies of state provision; and for those who leave home because they cannot get on with their families. For those in temporary or inadequate accommodation; for those in hostels; for those sleeping rough on the streets. **Bidding/Response.**

2) For those we call scroungers or beggars; for those obliged to practise deceit in order to gain our sympathy. **Bidding/ Response.**

3) For those who have homes, but are lonely within them, waiting for guests; For those who are too proud or reserved to share their lives with others. **Bidding/Response.**

4) For those who spend a lot of time with other people and do the social round, but never get to know anybody very well. **Bidding/Response.**

5) For those with fears and phobias that prevent close relationships; For those who suffer nightmares and are

always tired or under-the-weather. **Bidding/Response.**

6) For those who doubt - the goodness of life, themselves or the good intentions of others. **Bidding/Response.**

Traditional Hymn e.g. Lord Jesus in the days of old (A.J. Noble); Abide with me (H.F. Light)

The Meal.

Leader: 'As they came near to the village, Jesus walked on, as if he intended to continue his journey. But they would not hear of it. They insisted, "You must stay at our place. It's nearly night; there's no light left for travelling." We open our hearts to welcome Jesus.

Response: He accepts our invitation.

L: Jesus sits with us at table.

R: We will share our food with him.

L: 'When they were having supper, Jesus took a piece of bread, said 'thank you' to God.'

All: Thankyou God for these gifts, which come from you with love. Use us, like them, to show the new life brought by Jesus, your Likeness.

L: 'Then Jesus broke the bread and handed it to them.'

(The bread is broken, handed round, and retained by each, ready to eat together)

L: 'At that moment they realized who he was'

(All eat the bread)

Bidding: Jesus is risen! **Response:** He is risen indeed!

L: 'The two told the others how they had met Jesus on the road, and how they had recognized him when he broke the bread. While they were talking, they suddenly realized that Jesus was there with them. Jesus said, "Keep Calm, everybody!"

Bidding: Be at peace! **Response:** The same to you!

(All greet one another affectionately)

L: 'Jesus let them have a good look at his hands and his feet. They were very happy to see him, but still found it difficult to believe. Jesus said, "I could do with something to eat." They brought him some grilled fish and part of a honeycomb. He took the food and ate it while they watched.'

(Fish or biscuit in the shape of a fish and honeycomb handed round and shared. Or the honeycomb may be given to new members.)

Bidding: Jesus is risen! **Response:** He sure is!

L: This is what Rocky said at the home of Neil the Roman soldier: 'God gave the power of the Spirit to Jesus from Nazareth. He went everywhere doing good, and healing people from very severe illnesses. It was obvious that God was with him. We saw everything he did, in and around Jerusalem. They killed him by hanging him on a wooden post. But God brought him back to life three days later, and made it possible for him to be seen, not in public, but by a group of us specially chosen to tell other people afterwards. We actually ate and drank with Jesus after he returned to life.' (Luke's Good News Part Two, i.e. Acts: 10:38)

(The cup is presented ands then passed round)

L: Jesus is risen!

R: We know!

Hymn

MAY THE MIND (As in chapter five)

L: Jesus is risen!

R: Nothing's more certain!

All Together: The beauty of Jesus our Leader, the Love of God our Parent, and the Joy of the Spirit our Uniter be with us for ever.

APPENDIX SEVEN

COMMUNION ON THE SEA SHORE

(Suitable for Easter and the following late Spring and Summer months. (This Communion takes place **in the context** of an Easter Breakfast. The breakfast may take place before or after the communion.)

Scripture Sentence: Jesus said, "How would you like to be my friends and fish for people?" (Mark 1: 16)

Hymn Lord of the Dance (Sidney Carter)

Prayer God of the morning, of the new day, of new beginnings and fresh hopes, we worship you.

God who meets us in Jesus, risen from the dead, bearing still the marks of love, greeting us with open arms, we adore you.

Help us to recognize you when you beckon to us; help us to understand when you instruct us; help us to throw off our guilt when you forgive us; help us to love you when you ask us for our love.

We want to know Jesus, your proof to us of what you are.

Readings

Hebrew Scriptures Ezekiel 47: 6-12

Psalm 40 or 116

Christian Scriptures Sources Close to Jesus 21 (Gospel of John)

Post-Biblical Scriptures. e.g.

'..all deep understanding of Christ's meaning depends on seeing this. It is easy to make a hero of Jesus, as though that category could sum up his meaning. Well, he is a hero! It is easy to describe Jesus as a spiritual genius; his profound influence on human thought suggests that category. Well, he is a genius! It is easy to make an ideal of him; his personal quality, far ahead of us like a pillar of cloud by day and of fire by night, suggests that category. Well, he is the ideal! But when we have called him hero, genius, ideal, or what you will, we must go far beyond that if we are to apprehend his meaning. He is Savior, the heart and center of a rescue story.' (H.E. Fosdick 'On being fit to live with')

Hymn
I come with joy (Brian Wren)

Prayer: God of mercy and understanding, we pray for all who feel their work to be pointless or themselves to be a failure; for those who, even in the light of the Resurrection morning are frustrated or anxious or insecure. We pray for all who carry burdens of guilt for real or imagined offences, from the distant past or from recent events. We pray for those who seek to love and yet whose energies and emotions fail to rise to the demands that love makes upon them. We pray for those who earnestly seek to be better people than they are and yet somehow cannot make it; for those who want to follow you, but are afraid of the consequences in terms of the sacrifices they may be expected to make or the pain they may be called to endure.

We pray also for those who are very confident they have got it right, that they are doing your will and working effectively for you, that they may be given the humility to remember that without you they can do nothing. Give them the sensitivity to re-examine their performance in the pure light of your love, and the honesty to recognize they are part of the problem you wish to address.

Take each one aside, Jesus, our friend, and speak the words of questioning and calming, judgement and encouragement, rebuke and confidence, that our state of mind as we face our future may reflect the joy of the Good News and the inner peace that is your unique gift.

Traditional Hymn

Hark my soul, it is the Lord (Cowper) or Break thou the bread of life (Mary Lathbury)

Presider: 'When they came to the beach, they saw a barbecue fire with some fish being cooked, and some bread beside it…Jesus said, "Time for breakfast!"

Prayer (Together)

Jesus, we join you at your board.
Be here and everywhere adored:
These good things share, and grant that we
Your banquet full may one day see.

(Said or sung to Rimington or Old 100th)

Presider: 'Jesus came close to them, took the bread and gave it to them. Then he handed round the fish.

(Presider takes a portion of bread and a portion of fish and breaks each, then places it on plates where pieces of bread and fish are already placed on opposite sides, not touching. The plates are then handed round)

'Rocky *later* preached these words: "God brought Jesus back to life, and made it possible for him to be seen by a group of us specially chosen to tell other people afterwards. We ate and drank with Jesus after he returned to life." (Luke's Good News Part Two, i.e. Acts: 10:38)

(Fruit juice is passed around)

'None of the friends needed to ask Jesus, "What's your name?" they knew it was their Leader.'

Prayer: God made known to us in Jesus, thank you for looking upon us as your friends. We want to stay in company with you, to help you in your work, to enjoy your fullness of life, to share your heartaches, to love you and all people.

Hymn One morning on that misty shore (Pratt Green)

Bidding: Keep close to Jesus! **Response:** And you!